SAFETY AND ENVIRONMENTAL HEALTH

MACMILLAN

HEALTH

ENCYCLOPEDIA

8

SAFETY AND ENVIRONMENTAL HEALTH

MACMILLAN HEALTH ENCYCLOPEDIA

8

MACMILLAN PUBLISHING COMPANY
NEW YORK

MAXWELL MACMILLAN CANADA
TORONTO

MAXWELL MACMILLAN INTERNATIONAL
NEW YORK   OXFORD   SINGAPORE   SYDNEY

EDITORIAL CREDITS

Developed and produced by
Visual Education Corporation, Princeton, NJ

Project Editor: Darryl Kestler

Editors: Richard Bohlander, Susan Garver, Michael Gee, Emilie McCardell, Cynthia Mooney, Suzanne Murdico, Frances Wiser

Editorial Assistant: Carol Ciaston

Photo Editors: Maryellen Costa, Michael Gee

Photo Research: Cynthia Cappa, Sara Matthews

Production Supervisor: Anita Crandall

Proofreading Management: Amy Davis

Art Editors: Maureen Pancza, Mary Lyn Sodano

Advisor, Anatomical Illustrations:
David Seiden, Ph.D.
Robert Wood Johnson Medical School
Piscataway, New Jersey

Layout: Maxson Crandall, Lisa Evans

Word Processing: Cynthia Feldner

Design: Hespenheide Design

The information contained in the *Macmillan Health Encyclopedia* is not intended to take the place of the care and advice of a physician or health-care professional. Readers should obtain professional advice in making health-care decisions.

PHOTO CREDITS

Jacket: Howard Sochurek/The Stock Market

Ken Graham: 61

Howard M. Paul Communications: 54

Courtesy of Huntington Beach Marine Safety: 27

David Madison: 43

Mary E. Messenger: 67

mga/Photri: 100

Cliff Moore: 23, 30, 49, 58, 73, 80

PhotoEdit: 82; Bill Aron, 86; Robert Brenner, 83; Paul Conklin, 66; Amy Etra, 4, 88; Tony Freeman, 8, 16, 40, 56, 60, 91; Robert W. Ginn, 41; Richard Hutchings, 78, 79; Stephen McBrady, 22; Michael Newman, 33, 36; Elena Rooraid, 99; Rhoda Sidney, 32; Ulrike Welsch, 84; David Young-Wolff, 14, 65, 74, 75, 95; Elizabeth Zuckerman, 81

Photo Options: Bachmann, 94

Terry Wild Studio: 47

Tom Stack & Associates: Gary Milburn, 13

Unicorn Stock Photos: David Cummings, 64

U.S. Department of Labor/OSHA/OICA: E. Latour Photography, 63

Courtesy of Volvo: 12

Macmillan Publishing Company
866 Third Avenue
New York, NY 10022

Maxwell Macmillan Canada, Inc.
1200 Eglinton Avenue East, Suite 200
Don Mills, Ontario M3C 3N1

Macmillan Publishing Company is part of the Maxwell Communication Group of Companies

Printed in the United States of America

printing number
2 3 4 5 6 7 8 9 10

Library of Congress Cataloging-in-Publication Data

Macmillan health encyclopedia.
   v. <1–   >
   Includes index.
   Contents: v. 1. Body systems—v. 2. Communicable diseases—v. 3. Noncommunicable diseases and disorders—v. 4 Nutrition and fitness—v. 5. Emotional and mental health—v. 6. Sexuality and reproduction—v. 7. Drugs, alcohol, and tobacco—v. 8. Safety and environmental health—v. 9. Health-care systems/cumulative index
   ISBN 0-02-897439-5 (set).—ISBN 0-02-897431-X (v. 1).—ISBN 0-02-897432-8 (v. 2).
   1. Health—Encyclopedias.   I. Macmillan Publishing Company.
RA776.M174   1993
610´ .3—dc20   92-28939
                                     CIP

Volumes of the *Macmillan Health Encyclopedia*

1 *Body Systems* (ISBN 0-02-897431-X)
2 *Communicable Diseases* (ISBN 0-02-897432-8)
3 *Noncommunicable Diseases and Disorders* (ISBN 0-02-897433-6)
4 *Nutrition and Fitness* (ISBN 0-02-897434-4)
5 *Emotional and Mental Health* (ISBN 0-02-897435-2)
6 *Sexuality and Reproduction* (ISBN 0-02-897436-0)
7 *Drugs, Alcohol, and Tobacco* (ISBN 0-02-897437-9)
8 *Safety and Environmental Health* (ISBN 0-02-897438-7)
9 *Health-Care Systems/Cumulative Index* (ISBN 0-02-897453-0)

The *Macmillan Health Encyclopedia* is a nine-volume set that explains how the body works; describes the causes and treatment of hundreds of diseases and disorders; provides information on diet and exercise for a healthy lifestyle; discusses key issues in emotional, mental, and sexual health; covers problems relating to the use and abuse of legal and illegal drugs; outlines first-aid procedures; and provides up-to-date information on current health issues.

Written with the support of a distinguished panel of editorial advisors, the encyclopedia puts considerable emphasis on the idea of wellness. It discusses measures an individual can take to prevent illness and provides information about healthy lifestyle choices.

The *Macmillan Health Encyclopedia* is organized topically. Each of the nine volumes relates to an area covered in the school health curriculum. The encyclopedia also supplements course work in biology, psychology, home economics, and physical education. The volumes are organized as follows: 1. *Body Systems: Anatomy and Physiology;*   2. *Communicable Diseases: Symptoms, Diagnosis, Treatment;*   3. *Noncommunicable Diseases and Disorders: Symptoms, Diagnosis, Treatment;*   4. *Nutrition and Fitness;*   5. *Emotional and Mental Health;*   6. *Sexuality and Reproduction;*   7. *Drugs, Alcohol, and Tobacco;*   8. *Safety and Environmental Health;*   9. *Health-Care Systems/Cumulative Index.*

The information in the *Macmillan Health Encyclopedia* is clearly presented and easy to find. Entries are arranged in alphabetical order within each volume. An extensive system of cross-referencing directs the reader from a synonym to the main entry (GERMAN MEASLES see RUBELLA) and from one entry to additional information in other entries. Words printed in SMALL CAPITALS ("These substances, found in a number of NONPRESCRIPTION DRUGS . . .") indicate that there is an entry of that name in the volume. Most entries end with a list of "see also" cross-references to related topics. Entries within the same volume have no number (See also ANTI-INFLAMMATORY DRUGS); entries located in another volume include the volume number (See also HYPERTENSION, 3). All topics covered in a volume can be found in the index at the back of the book. There is also a comprehensive index to the set in Volume 9.

The extensive use of illustration includes colorful drawings, photographs, charts, and graphs to supplement and enrich the information presented in the text.

Questions of particular concern to the reader—When should I see a doctor? What are the risk factors? What can I do to prevent an illness?—are indicated by the following marginal notations: Consult a Physician, Risk Factors, and Healthy Choices.

Although difficult terms are explained within the context of the entry, each volume of the encyclopedia also has its own GLOSSARY. Located in the front of the book, the glossary provides brief definitions of medical or technical terms with which the reader may not be familiar.

A SUPPLEMENTARY SOURCES section at the back of the book contains a listing of suggested reading material, as well as organizations from which additional information can be obtained.

GLOSSARY

acute Refers to a symptom or disease that begins suddenly, is usually severe, and generally lasts a short time.

artery A blood vessel that carries blood away from the heart.

asphyxiation Loss of consciousness, and possibly death, resulting from too little oxygen in the blood. Drowning and suffocation are examples of death by asphyxia.

bacteria (sing. *bacterium*) Single-celled, microscopic organisms, abundant in living things, air, soil, and water. Some are beneficial to humans, while others cause disease (see MICRO-ORGANISMS, **2**).

biodegradable Refers to products that will decompose completely and return to a natural state within a reasonably short period of time.

bloodstream The blood flowing through the veins, arteries, and capillaries.

blood vessels A general term for the arteries, veins, and capillaries through which blood circulates in the body.

carcinogen Any agent capable of causing cancer, such as tobacco tars, radiation, and certain chemicals.

cartilage Strong, dense, elastic tissue found in the nose, ears, and joints (see CONNECTIVE TISSUE, **1**).

central nervous system (CNS) The brain and spinal cord, the control center for all bodily functions.

chronic Refers to a disorder or set of symptoms that persists over a period of time or recurs frequently. Asthma and hypertension are chronic conditions.

concussion Disruption of brain function due to a blow or fall, causing brief unconsciousness.

conservation Systematic protection, preservation, and controlled use of natural resources, such as forests and water.

dehydration Excessive loss of water from the body.

disease, disorder An abnormal change in the structure or functioning of an organ or system in the body that produces a set of symptoms. The change may be caused by infection, heredity, injury, environment, or lifestyle or by a combination of these.

food chain Interdependence of various organisms that feed on the members below. Examples of the food chain include hawk, snake, frog, and insect; fox, rabbit, and grass; human, cow, and grass.

geothermal energy Energy produced by heat from the earth's interior layers of molten rock.

hemorrhage Severe, uncontrolled bleeding, either internal or external.

histamine A chemical compound released by body tissues during an allergic reaction, causing blood vessels to dilate.

hydrocarbons Chemical compounds containing hydrogen and carbon that are released into the air from the burning of gasoline and other fossil fuels. Hydrocarbons help create smog and other types of air pollution.

infection A condition caused by bacteria, viruses, fungi, or other microorganisms that invade and damage body cells and tissue.

infectious Refers to a disease that can spread (see COMMUNICABLE DISEASE, **2**).

inflammation Redness, swelling, pain, and heat in a body tissue due to physical injury, infection, or irritation.

lifestyle The way a person lives, as shown by attitudes, habits, and behavior.

microorganism Any plant or animal so small that it can be seen only through a microscope.

organism Any plant or animal.

pathogen A microorganism, such as a bacterium or a virus, that can cause disease.

pollutant Any substance or energy—often a by-product of human society—

that causes a negative effect on the environment.

pulmonary Pertaining to the lungs.

radioactivity The property of certain elements, such as uranium, that causes them to release particles or rays of energy from changes in the nuclei (sing. *nucleus*) of their atoms.

seizure A sudden attack, usually marked by convulsions and loss of consciousness, such as occurs with epilepsy.

shock The body's reaction to a sudden, strong disturbance, marked by the lowering of blood pressure, pulse, and other vital signs. The inadequate blood flow may result in physical failure.

spasm Involuntary and abnormal muscular contraction.

stress The body's response to any physical or mental demand made on it.

symptom A change in normal body function indicating the presence of a disease or disorder. A sore throat is a symptom of infection.

tendon A tough, flexible, fibrous cord that joins muscle to a bone or muscle to muscle in the body.

trauma A physical or emotional shock that damages or upsets the body.

tumor Any abnormal mass of body tissue that forms when cells reproduce at a rapid rate. Tumors are benign or malignant (cancerous).

vascular Pertaining to the blood vessels and the circulation of blood through the body.

vertebrae (sing. *vertebra*) The bony segments of the spinal column.

virus The smallest known living infectious agent (see MICROORGANISMS, 2).

vital signs Indicators, such as pulse, temperature, and respiration, that the body is functioning.

wellness A state of physical, mental, and social well-being that allows a person to function at his or her best.

ACCESS FOR PEOPLE WITH DISABILITIES

Access for people with disabilities involves modifications to public and private facilities. These adaptations to buildings, furniture, and various appliances can help people with physical disabilities function more easily and independently at home, at work, and in everyday situations.

The Americans with Disabilities Act, a law passed in 1990 and which went into effect in 1992, protects people who are physically disabled against discrimination. The Act also requires that public accommodations, retail establishments, and newly built public transportation vehicles be accessible to these individuals. In addition, many organizations provide special resources for the physically disabled who want to travel independently or participate in activities such as dance, music, and sports.

Hearing and Speech Impairments   A variety of devices can help people with hearing or speech impairments. For example, sign language at lectures and cultural events and *closed captioning* for television make it possible for people with hearing impairments to enjoy the events and programs. TT (Text Telephone) telecommunications systems (also called TTY or TDD systems) include typewriterlike devices that enable people with speech and hearing impairments to communicate by telephone. Other useful adaptations include doorbells and telephones equipped with signal lights to indicate ringing.

Visual Impairments   Homes for the visually impaired need to have clear passages. Braille knobs and control panels can easily be installed on appliances. Outside the home, braille allows people who are visually impaired to read items like menus and elevator control panels. A broad selection of audiotaped readings of books is available for blind people from libraries and organizations such as Recording for the Blind, Inc. In addition, reading machines can transform a page of printed words into spoken words.

Access for Wheelchairs   People who use wheelchairs have unique needs. One of the most important is access ramps, which are required for

Increasing Access. *Lowered curbs and building ramps enable people who use wheelchairs to move around more independently.*

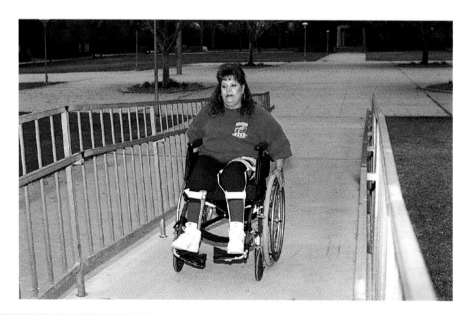

new public buildings and can be added to existing houses and apartment buildings. Other space requirements include wide, clear doorways and hallways and ample turning space. Door handles, closet rods, light switches, thermostats, mirrors, and telephones may need to be lowered to be within easy reach. Bathrooms can be equipped with wheel-in showers and higher-than-normal toilets with grab bars. Lower-than-usual counter-tops, sinks, and ranges with room below for knees and the wheelchair can be built. A special lift may be installed in a house to allow wheelchairs to go up and down between floors. Some of these modifications are also useful for people who use crutches or a walker.

ACCIDENTS

RISK FACTORS
▶ ▶ ▶ ▶ ▶ ▶

Accidents, or unintentional injuries, are the leading cause of death and disability among young and middle-aged Americans. They also annually kill or injure a significant number of elderly people. On the highways, in the home, and in the workplace, accidents claim thousands of lives every year and cost the nation billions of dollars in medical treatment and lost worker productivity. Most accidents result from unsafe behavior or equipment, an unsafe environment, or a combination of these factors. And most accidents could be prevented.

Types of Accidents Motor vehicle accidents account for roughly half of all accidental deaths. Lower speed limits, safety belt use, and tough drunk-driving laws have led to a reduction in automobile deaths over the past 20 years, but, nevertheless, more than 46,000 people died in motor vehicle accidents in 1990 (see graph: Main Types of Accidental Deaths, 1990). And at least half of the fatal automobile accidents involved alcohol.

RISK FACTORS
▶ ▶ ▶ ▶ ▶ ▶

Each year, more than 20,000 people die, and more than a million are seriously disabled, in accidents in the home. Among the most common types of home accidents are falls, fires, and poisoning. The age groups most often affected are children and elderly people. Burns account for the greatest number of deaths among children, whereas falls account for the majority of accidents among the elderly.

Thanks to safety legislation and safer equipment and machinery, the number of workplace accidents has declined significantly since the beginning of this century. Nevertheless, thousands of Americans die in work-related accidents each year. The majority of these accidents involve manual labor. Occupational areas that put workers at particular risk of accidents include construction, agriculture, fire fighting, forestry, and mining.

RISK FACTORS
▶ ▶ ▶ ▶ ▶ ▶

Why Accidents Happen Although accidents may appear to happen by chance, studies suggest that a variety of factors often interact to cause an accident. Unsafe behavior is one such factor. It includes driving under the influence of alcohol or drugs, ignoring speed limits or safety devices like safety belts or bicycle helmets, or operating equipment without the proper knowledge.

Another factor that can lead to an accident is unsafe equipment. For example, an automobile with worn tires is more likely to skid on a wet road. A blunt kitchen knife is more likely to slip and cut someone.

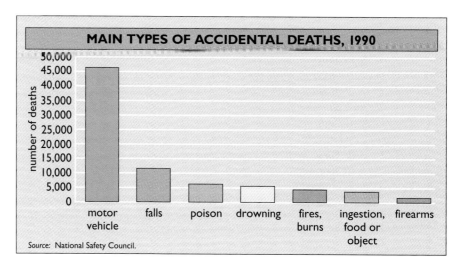

MAIN TYPES OF ACCIDENTAL DEATHS, 1990

Source: National Safety Council.

A third factor is an unsafe environment. A driver is more likely to have an accident on a wet and slippery road. An elderly person is more likely to fall in a slippery bathtub. A child is more likely to suffer suffocation or poisoning in a home in which plastic bags and household chemicals are left within reach.

Preventing Accidents Knowing what can cause accidents is the first step toward preventing them. Every individual can take certain steps to reduce the risk of an accident. These *active prevention* measures include wearing safety belts while driving or riding in a car, never drinking and driving, wearing bicycle and motorcycle helmets, and keeping poisonous substances out of the reach of children. Educating people about safety risks and the penalties imposed for certain behaviors can also help prevent accidents.

Another effective way of reducing accidents is through *passive prevention*—the use of safety devices that require little or no effort from the individual concerned. Examples of passive safety devices include air bags and automatic safety belts in cars, built-in safety switches on power tools, and bright street lighting.

Over the past few decades, efforts to reduce accident rates have had some success, but there is still a long way to go. Although automobile manufacturers must by law include passive safety features in their products, both government and industry have been slow to legislate and implement comprehensive safety measures. For the most part, it is up to the individual to identify potential hazards in products and in the environment and to examine the ways in which his or her own behavior contributes to the risk of an accident. (See also AUTOMOBILE SAFETY; BICYCLE SAFETY; ELECTRICAL SAFETY; HOME SAFETY; MOTORCYCLE SAFETY; WATER SAFETY.)

HEALTHY CHOICES

► **ACID RAIN**

Acid rain is a type of WATER POLLUTION that occurs when pollutants released during the burning of FOSSIL FUELS combine with moisture in the air and fall back to earth as rain with a high acidic content. When acid rain collects in lakes and rivers, it raises the level of acidity in the water, eventually damaging or killing the aquatic life. Acid rain also destroys the

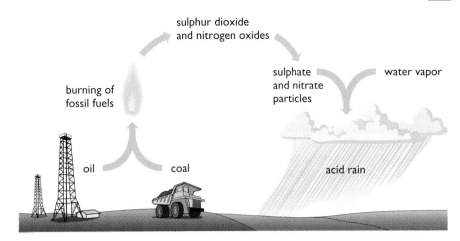

How Acid Rain Is Produced.
When fossil fuels such as coal and oil are burned to produce energy, sulphur dioxide and nitrogen oxides are emitted into the air. Here sulphate and nitrate particles are formed. These particles mix with water vapor and fall to the earth as acid rain, which damages plants and wildlife and may harm humans.

roots and leaves of trees, damages crops, and affects the mineral content of the soil. Some of the particles that form acid rain may also be linked to respiratory diseases in humans.

How Acid Rain Is Formed   Sulphur dioxide and nitrogen oxides, the chemicals responsible for acid rain, are created as a result of a variety of industrial processes. The major source of *sulphur dioxide* is the burning of coal. *Nitrogen oxides* are produced by gasoline-powered vehicles as well as by coal-burning utilities and other kinds of industry. As particles of sulphur dioxide and nitrogen oxides travel through the air, they combine with water vapor to form nitric and sulphuric acids. Eventually these chemicals fall to earth as precipitation.

In the United States, acid rain occurs most often in the northeastern and midwestern states, where emissions of sulphur dioxide and nitrogen oxides are highest. However, winds may carry the pollutants hundreds or even thousands of miles before they fall as acidic dew, drizzle, fog, sleet, snow, or rain. (See also AIR POLLUTION; PARTICULATES.)

▶ AGRICULTURAL POLLUTION
Agricultural pollution is caused by the use of chemicals to increase crop yields and eliminate weeds and insect pests. Many of these substances can be very damaging to wildlife and, if they enter the food chain or water supplies, can also pose a serious threat to human health.

Chemical Use in Agriculture   Each year in the United States, hundreds of millions of pounds of *agricultural chemicals*—in the form of fertilizers, pesticides, herbicides, and fungicides—are used on farms and on home lawns and gardens. *Fertilizers* are used to increase crop yields and make lawns and garden plants grow better. *Pesticides* are used to kill insect pests and rodents, which can pose a major threat to agriculture. *Herbicides* help kill unwanted weeds. *Fungicides* help prevent *fungal diseases* that can wipe out entire crops. (See also AGRICULTURAL CHEMICALS, **4.**)

Agricultural Pollution   The introduction of agricultural chemicals in the twentieth century has revolutionized farming by making it possible to produce a larger, more reliable, and more appealing food supply. However,

Dangerous Chemicals. *Many of the chemicals that help crops grow and protect them from insect pests and diseases are also potentially harmful to humans.*

their widespread use has also posed many environmental and safety concerns. A primary concern is for the long-term effects of toxic chemicals within an ECOSYSTEM. In 1972, the federal government banned the use of DDT, a potent pesticide, because of strong evidence that it was killing birds and other wildlife. Federal regulations now control the testing and use of pesticides and other agricultural chemicals, but their long-term environmental impact—especially when several are used together—may be impossible to estimate.

Other concerns are for the direct effects of agricultural chemicals on humans. Some toxic chemicals have proved harmful to agricultural workers, and the Environmental Protection Agency has developed regulations to protect workers from exposure to pesticides. In addition, the residue on fruits and vegetables may be harmful to consumers, and possible contamination of water supplies is a problem. After agricultural chemicals are added to crops, rain or irrigation systems often wash them into waterways, contributing to WATER POLLUTION.

Reducing Agricultural Pollution A variety of methods have been suggested to lessen the impact of agricultural chemicals on the environment. One way to control insect pests, for example, is through biological or natural control—by using the natural enemies of pests or natural pesticides derived from plants. Instead of using chemical fertilizers, organic fertilizers like cattle manure and compost can be used. Farming practices such as crop rotation can also help reduce the need for chemical fertilizers. For home gardens and lawns, hand weeding and mulching are safe alternatives to chemical herbicides.

HEALTHY CHOICES
●●●●●●●●●●●●●

Washing fruits and vegetables before eating them will help to remove chemicals from the outside of the produce. Many consumers are choosing to buy produce grown organically—without chemical pesticides and fungicides—to protect their health. (See also TOXIC SUBSTANCES; ORGANIC FOOD, 4.)

▷ **AIR BAGS**   see AUTOMOBILE SAFETY

▷ **AIR POLLUTION**   Air pollution is the presence of various gases and tiny particles in the air that can harm human health and damage the environment. Some air pollution is caused by natural processes, such as plant pollination, forest fires, and volcanic eruptions. The most damaging air pollution, however, is caused by human activities, especially the burning of FOSSIL FUELS (coal, oil, and natural gas).

The two major types of pollutants in the air are *gaseous pollutants* and *particulate pollutants*. Among the most common gaseous pollutants are CARBON DIOXIDE, carbon monoxide, hydrocarbons, nitrogen oxides, sulphur oxides, and OZONE. PARTICULATES, which are tiny particles of matter suspended in the air, include dust, ash, and other fine materials such as ASBESTOS fibers and LEAD particles.

Sources of Air Pollution   The burning of fossil fuels in motor vehicles, power plants, and factories is the major cause of the gaseous pollutants that damage the environment. Gaseous pollutants are also produced indoors by cigarette smoking, furnaces, and gas ranges, as well as by certain construction materials, cleaning products, and home furnishings. Another gaseous pollutant, RADON, comes from the earth itself. It is a radioactive gas produced by the natural decay of radium.

Particulates also come from a variety of sources, ranging from flowering plants (pollen) and mold spores to the asbestos released from deteriorating insulation or fireproofing materials. Some particulates, such as lead, are produced by motor vehicle emissions; others are the by-products of industrial processes and mining.

Effects of Air Pollution   Air pollution can be damaging to human health and the environment. The most immediate threat to human health is to the body's respiratory system. Many pollutants irritate the throat and nasal passages, damage the lungs, and impair respiration. Elderly people and people with respiratory problems such as asthma are at greater risk than others.

RISK FACTORS
▶ ▶ ▶ ▶ ▶ ▶

Pollutants can also irritate the eyes and cause headaches and fatigue. By interfering with the blood's ability to carry oxygen, pollutants like carbon monoxide can contribute to heart disease. Concentrated exposure to carbon monoxide can cause unconsciousness or death. Prolonged exposure to some pollutants has been linked to cancer. The dangers of air pollution can be especially great during periods when SMOG, visible air pollution, hangs over cities as a result of a TEMPERATURE INVERSION. At such times, pollutants are trapped near the ground and may accumulate to especially dangerous levels. (See also CARBON MONOXIDE POISONING; ASTHMA, **3**; HEART DISEASE, **3**; LUNG DISEASE, **3**.)

In addition to its effects on human health, some forms of air pollution damage the environment. The buildup of carbon dioxide in the atmosphere, for example, is thought to be a major factor in GLOBAL WARMING. Nitrogen oxides and sulphur oxides combine with oxygen and

The Pollution Standards Index.
The pollution standards index collects data on a number of pollutants throughout an urban area. The index is represented as a single number ranging from 0 to 500. Local television and radio news programs often report the PSI to their audiences.

THE POLLUTION STANDARDS INDEX

PSI range	Description
0–50	Good
51–100	Moderate
101–199	Unhealthy
200–299	Very unhealthy
300–500	Hazardous

atmospheric moisture to produce ACID RAIN, which damages forests and the plant and animal life of lakes. Substances called chlorofluorocarbons (CFCs) are capable of destroying the *ozone layer* in the upper atmosphere. This gaseous layer protects plant and animal life against the harmful effects of ultraviolet rays from the sun. Each of these environmental effects in turn has negative consequences for human health.

Dealing with Air Pollution   Although some progress has been made to improve air quality, there is still much to be accomplished. In the United States, laws such as the Clean Air Acts are aimed at monitoring polluters and controlling the amount of pollutants released into the atmosphere.

HEALTHY CHOICES
●●●●●●●●●●●●●

It is wise for individuals to be aware of the pollution around them and to take steps to lessen its effects on their health. Many physicians suggest that people avoid exercising outside when pollutant levels are high. The Environmental Protection Agency (EPA) has created a *pollution standards index* (PSI) to determine when air is unsafe to breathe (see chart: The Pollution Standards Index). People with allergies also need to be aware of the *pollen count*, which determines the average number of pollen grains in the air in a particular place over a period of time. The pollen count is often provided as part of the local weather report on television and radio news programs and in the newspaper.

▶ ARTIFICIAL RESPIRATION   see CPR

▶ ASBESTOS

Asbestos is a lightweight, fireproof mineral once widely used in construction materials and insulation products. It separates easily into nearly indestructible microscopic fibers. These fibers can lodge in the lungs and cause chronic lung diseases that include *asbestosis*, a permanent lung inflammation, and cancer. Since the 1970s, asbestos has not been widely used in building materials. A national effort costing billions of dollars is under way to remove asbestos from public buildings.

People who work with asbestos today must wear special protective suits and masks to avoid inhaling asbestos fibers. Most experts believe that asbestos in the home is not dangerous unless it is crumbling. In such cases, the asbestos should be removed or sealed by professionals. (See also PARTICULATES; CARCINOGENS, **3**; LUNG DISEASE, **3**.)

▶ AUTOMOBILE SAFETY

Automobile safety involves laws, equipment, driving skills, and precautions that can help avoid accidents or prevent injury and death in an accident. About 50,000 Americans are killed in automobile accidents every year, and almost 2 million more are injured. Motor vehicle accidents are the most common cause of death among people younger than the age of 35 and the major cause of accidental death for people of all ages. Drivers younger than age 25 have more accidents than any other age group and are particularly vulnerable to injury and death. The following are important considerations in exercising automobile safety.

Safety Features Most cars are equipped with features designed to protect passengers from serious injury in a collision. Among the most important are *seat belts*, which protect against head and spinal injuries, the most common injuries sustained in automobile accidents. Wearing a seat belt reduces the chance of being seriously injured by 50 percent and the chance of being killed by 60 to 70 percent. Using seat belts is required by law in most states; however, only 50 percent of Americans buckle up on a regular basis. It is estimated that 12,000 to 16,000 lives could be saved annually if everyone used seat belts for every trip. Drivers should make sure that they and all passengers wear seat belts, even when traveling only a short distance (see graph: Lives Saved by Seat Belts, 1983–1990).

HEALTHY CHOICES

HEALTHY CHOICES

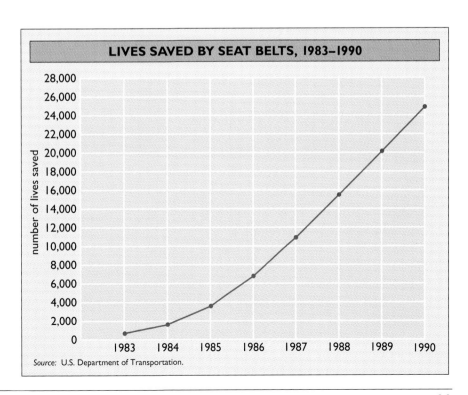

LIVES SAVED BY SEAT BELTS, 1983–1990

number of lives saved

Source: U.S. Department of Transportation.

Crash Dummies. *Technically complex dummies are used to test the design and safety features of automobiles in various types of collisions.*

Many older cars have seat belts that are user-controlled—that is, belts which the occupant is responsible for engaging. Since 1989, however, federal safety standards have required that all new cars sold in the United States have *passive restraints*, which protect passengers automatically. Passive restraints can be either automatic seat belts, which are attached to the car seat and door, an air bag, or both. An *air bag* inflates instantly in the event of a front-end impact, preventing the passenger from hitting the dashboard or windshield. Air bags do not eliminate the need for seat belts, however. In fact, their effectiveness depends on the ability of seat belts to hold occupants in place during an accident. By 1997, all new cars are to be equipped with a driver-side air bag.

Most states also require that infants and children ride in specially designed *car seats*. Children younger than 4 years of age who are not protected by a special seat are 11 times more likely to be killed in an accident than are children who are riding in safety seats.

Drinking, Drugs, and Driving Driving under the influence of alcohol, illegal drugs, or even certain medications impairs coordination and reflexes and significantly increases the chance of motor vehicle injury. Never drive an automobile after drinking alcohol. Half of all fatal automobile crashes involve drivers who have been drinking, and alcohol-related motor vehicle accidents kill more than 23,500 Americans every year.

Vehicle Maintenance Keeping cars in good repair and following the manufacturer's recommended maintenance schedule are essential for safe driving. Bald tires, poorly adjusted lights, and worn brakes are hazardous. Check the condition of the spare tire regularly. Make sure the lights, brakes, windshield wipers, and steering are working properly. Equip the car with a FIRST AID KIT and emergency flare or other signaling device.

HEALTHY CHOICES
● ● ● ● ● ● ● ● ● ● ●

Traffic Laws Traffic laws, signals, and markings are designed for safety. Always obey speed limits and traffic signals and signs, yield the right of way, and pass properly. Be especially careful at intersections and railway crossings. Improper driving practices, of which speeding is the major violation, account for about 72 percent of all car accidents.

Weather Conditions Rain, snow, and reduced visibility are potentially dangerous conditions, often deceptively so, that require a slower speed. In severe conditions, travel should be delayed until road conditions improve. Be prepared for emergencies: In very cold weather, carry food, blankets, and extra clothing.

HEALTHY CHOICES

Defensive Driving Driving defensively means thinking ahead and anticipating what could happen on the road. It is important to be aware of other drivers at all times and be prepared to take evasive action. Driving defensively involves several simple rules:

- Never challenge other drivers.
- Don't follow too closely—for every 10 miles per hour of speed, allow at least one car length in front.
- Keep all angles of visibility clear at all times by keeping windows and mirrors clean and free of accumulated objects.
- Learn where the mirror "blind spots" are in the vehicle.
- When changing lanes, pulling out from the curb, or turning, look to the rear to check for cars in addition to using rearview mirrors.
- Pay special attention to bicyclists, animals, pedestrians, runners, and motorcyclists.
- Don't be distracted by the radio, a conversation, or the scenery. Keep the radio volume tuned to a level that allows the traffic outside the car to be heard.
- Pay close attention to the road. (See also ACCIDENTS; BICYCLE SAFETY; MOTORCYCLE SAFETY; DRINKING AND DRIVING, 7.)

▶ BENDS

RISK FACTORS
▶ ▶ ▶ ▶ ▶ ▶

The bends is the common name for *decompression sickness,* a condition that occurs when a person goes from a high-pressure environment to a normal-pressure environment too rapidly. It most often affects deep-sea divers, deep-sea workers, and pilots. The change in pressure traps nitrogen bubbles in the blood and tissues, causing the tissues to stretch and

Decompression Chamber. *To avoid the bends, deep-sea workers enter a decompression chamber where they are gradually reaccustomed to normal atmospheric pressure.*

become painful. It is called the bends because it can cause sufferers to bend over in pain. In severe cases, it can result in convulsions and death.

Symptoms of the bends include severe pain in the bones and joints, chest tightness, nausea, vomiting, and giddiness. The bends can be prevented by moving slowly from a high-pressure atmosphere to an atmosphere of normal pressure. This gives the nitrogen in the bloodstream time to dissolve so that it can be exhaled through the lungs. The bends is prevented or treated by placing the person in a special decompression chamber (see illustration: Decompression Chamber) where the pressure is decreased gradually until the body's nitrogen level is restored to normal.

▶ BICYCLE SAFETY

Bicycle safety involves a number of precautions that can help prevent injury and death. Each year in the United States, cyclists are involved in more than a million serious accidents. More than half of these involve children younger than the age of 14. It is estimated that in 80 to 90 percent of bicycle accidents, the cyclist is at fault. The chances of a cycling accident can be greatly reduced by observing the following safety guidelines.

HEALTHY CHOICES

Safety Helmets. *A helmet is the single most important piece of safety equipment for a cyclist. Helmets come in a wide variety of styles and sizes.*

Wear Appropriate Cycling Gear Bicyclists should always wear protective helmets because head injuries are common, accounting for 75 percent of cycling fatalities. The helmet should have a durable outer shell and adjustable foam pads within to ensure a proper fit. Bright colored clothing or fluorescent vests can enhance the visibility of cyclists during the day and are even more important at night.

Follow Traffic Laws Bicyclists should ride in cycling lanes wherever possible. When on the road, they must stay to the right and ride in single file. Traffic laws that apply to motor vehicles also apply to cyclists. They must stop at stop signs, signal clearly, check for traffic before turning, and use extra caution in wet conditions.

Ride Defensively Bicyclists should try to make eye contact with other riders, drivers, and pedestrians, but they also need to be on the lookout for potholes and other hazards. They should always ride within their abilities and avoid unnecessary risks. Cyclists should not wear earphones while riding because they may not hear warning sounds from traffic.

Equip and Maintain the Bicycle Bicycles should have front and rear lights and special reflectors that motorists can see clearly. A bicycle that is used to carry a child should have a special seat with secure straps for young passengers. Children should never be allowed to ride on the handlebars. The bike should be kept clean and in good working order.

▶ BIOSPHERE

The biosphere is the vast region surrounding the earth's surface in which all living organisms are found. Encompassing the earth's crust, water, and atmosphere, the biosphere includes both the organisms and the nonliving substances (such as air, water, and soil) that surround them. Damage to

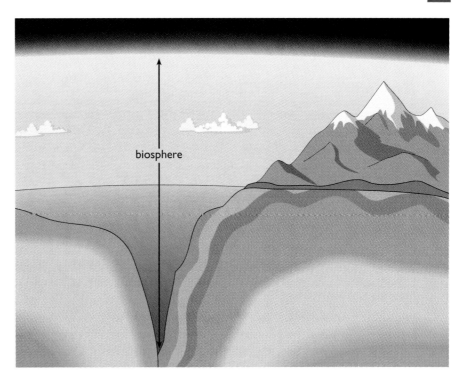

The Biosphere. *The biosphere includes all regions of the earth that can sustain life. These regions include the waters of the earth, the earth's surface and sediments of its crust, and the lower region of the atmosphere.*

the earth's biosphere can have a serious effect on the health and survival of plant and animal life, including human life.

The biosphere is sometimes referred to as a web of life because its components are interrelated. They are always interacting with each other within smaller, more self-contained ECOSYSTEMS. The substances that living things need for survival are continually cycled by such processes as photosynthesis and the circulation of air, water, and other kinds of matter. Disruption of these delicately balanced processes by natural events or human activities can disturb the ecosystems and threaten the survival of the organisms within them. Today, many experts are concerned about the environmental consequences of human activities. AIR POLLUTION, WATER POLLUTION, POPULATION GROWTH, and destruction of vital ecosystems like tropical rain forests are putting tremendous strains on the biosphere. Although the extent of damage varies from place to place, some experts fear that if current trends continue, the biosphere as a whole may be seriously harmed and could someday collapse.

Recently, there have been cooperative efforts by a number of nations to confront the problems facing the biosphere. Many experts wonder, however, whether enough will be done in time to prevent serious damage to the biosphere and to the health of humans and other living things. (See also ACID RAIN; GLOBAL WARMING; THERMAL POLLUTION.)

▶ BITES AND STINGS

Bites and stings from animals and insects can range in severity from mildly irritating to life threatening. In order to deal with bites and stings effectively, you need to know what kind of animal or insect inflicted the wound, how to treat the wound, what symptoms to look for, and when to see a physician.

Insect Stings. *For most people, a sting from a wasp or a bee is a painful, but short-lived, nuisance. For people who are particularly sensitive to stings, however, there is a danger of anaphylactic shock.*

Animal Bites The most common animal bites are those inflicted by pet cats and dogs. However, strays and wild animals such as raccoons, squirrels, and skunks also bite people. Even minor WOUNDS from animals can cause disease and should probably be seen by a physician. A minor animal bite should be cleaned thoroughly with soap and running water for at least 5 minutes. A more serious bite, such as one that breaks the skin or one involving a deep puncture wound (torn flesh), should be treated by a physician. The physician will clean and treat the wound and may give a tetanus shot.

CONSULT A PHYSICIAN

In certain parts of the United States, a bite from a wild animal, or from a domestic animal that is allowed to roam wild, carries the risk of *rabies*. Rabies is a viral infection that can be transmitted from animals to humans in saliva. If left untreated, it is fatal. If there is a risk of rabies, the animal that inflicted the bite should be caught, if possible, and kept under observation to determine whether the animal has the disease. If the animal cannot be caught, the physician must decide whether the bite victim should be treated for rabies.

Human bites that puncture the skin can be extremely dangerous. Bacteria in the mouth that enter the bloodstream of the bite victim can cause serious infections. Human bites that have broken the skin should always be referred to a physician immediately.

CONSULT A PHYSICIAN

Insect Bites and Stings Minor bites from insects such as mosquitoes, fleas, flies, bedbugs, ants, and chiggers cause pain, itching, swelling, and irritation. These symptoms result from venom that is injected into the skin, and they can last from a few hours to a few days. Bees, wasps, and yellow jackets can cause more serious reactions in people who are particularly sensitive to their stings.

Bee stings and insect bites are treated by carefully scraping the stinger away from the skin with a knifeblade or fingernail (if necessary), washing the area with soap and water, and applying a paste of baking soda, a wet cloth, or ice cubes to reduce pain. Over-the-counter hydrocortisone cream can help reduce itching and inflammation. Seek medical attention if the bite is serious or if symptoms of *anaphylactic shock* develop, such as difficulty in breathing, nausea, or dizziness. Severe reactions are treated by placing a constricting band 2 to 4 inches above the bite (if it occurred on a leg or arm). With a constricting band, a pulse can be felt below the band, and it is possible to slip a finger under the band. Keep the band in place, and seek medical help. (See also SHOCK, **3.**)

CONSULT A
PHYSICIAN

Tick bites require special treatment: Remove the tick carefully with tweezers, and wash the area thoroughly. Save the tick in a small, labeled container to show to the doctor if signs of infection develop. (See also LYME DISEASE, **2**; ROCKY MOUNTAIN SPOTTED FEVER, **2**; TICKS, **2.**)

RISK FACTORS
▶ ▶ ▶ ▶ ▶ ▶

Spider Bites Bites from nonpoisonous spiders can be treated in the same way as insect bites. Bites from poisonous spiders (like the black widow or brown recluse) are harmful, especially to young children and the elderly. Poisonous bites are treated by keeping the area of the bite lower than the heart to limit circulation of the venom and by applying ice or cold compresses to the area. If signs of anaphylactic shock develop and if breathing is affected, help maintain an open airway, and restore breathing if necessary by using artificial respiration or CPR. Seek medical assistance immediately. If possible, take the spider to the medical facility.

CONSULT A
PHYSICIAN

Snake Bites Most snakes are not poisonous. Nonpoisonous snake bites are treated by washing the bite area thoroughly and by applying antibiotic cream and a bandage. Rattlesnakes, coral snakes, water moccasins, and copperheads are poisonous. If a snakebite is painful and begins to swell or change color, the snake was probably poisonous. Poisonous bites are treated by lying quietly and holding the area lower than the heart. If the bite is on a leg or arm, place a constricting band a few inches above the bite, and watch for signs of anaphylactic shock. Seek medical assistance immediately. If possible, capture and kill the snake—without deforming its head—and take it to the medical facility. If this cannot be done, try to describe the snake to a physician.

CONSULT A
PHYSICIAN

Scorpion Stings Some species of scorpion are more poisonous than others. Symptoms of a sting may include severe pain or numbness and tingling at the site, nausea and vomiting, stomach pain, and muscle spasms. Scorpion stings are treated by keeping the area lower than the heart, applying ice or cold compresses, and seeking medical assistance immediately. If breathing is affected, maintain an open airway, and restore breathing if necessary by using artificial respiration.

Stings from Sea Creatures Jellyfish, Portuguese men-of-war, sea anemones, and some corals can sting by discharging toxin on contact with the skin. Symptoms include painful red welts, shortness of breath, nausea, and stomach cramps. More serious stings can cause anaphylactic shock, fainting, muscle cramps, vomiting, and difficulty in breathing. Fatal reactions occur but are rare. A person who has been stung by a jellyfish, Portuguese man-of-war, or sea anemone should get out of the water. The area of the sting should be treated by applying meat tenderizer, vinegar, salt, sugar, or dry sand and rubbing it gently. Clean the wound carefully with sea water—do not use fresh water, because it can activate stinging cells. Remove tentacles if necessary by wiping with a towel or gloved hand, and apply hydrocortisone cream or local anesthetic ointment. If the reaction is

CONSULT A PHYSICIAN

severe, seek medical assistance. For stings from coral or sea urchins, remove any fragments embedded in the skin, and wash the area with soap and water. (See also FIRST AID KIT; RABIES, **2**; TETANUS, **2**; INSECT REPELLENT, **7**.)

BLEEDING

Bleeding is any loss of blood from the body. *External bleeding* is caused by cuts, punctures, or other wounds; *internal bleeding* is caused by certain illnesses and severe trauma and occurs within the body. A large loss of blood, either externally or internally, can cause a dramatic drop in blood pressure and may be life threatening. Major bleeding is also called *hemorrhaging*. (See also BLOOD PRESSURE, **1**.)

External Bleeding The three main types of external bleeding are capillary bleeding, caused by minor cuts or scrapes; venous bleeding, which results from cuts that open veins and release dark red blood that flows steadily and slowly; and arterial bleeding, which occurs when an INJURY causes an artery to open, releasing bright red blood that spurts from the wound. Arterial bleeding is the most serious because a lot of blood can be lost very quickly. In fact, it is possible for arterial bleeding to result in death in as little as 1 minute.

First Aid for External Bleeding Anyone providing FIRST AID to a person who is bleeding should wash his or her hands before and after giving aid and wear rubber gloves whenever possible to prevent the spread of infection. Minor WOUNDS should be washed thoroughly with soap and water. First aid for a more serious injury involves applying direct pressure over the wound. If possible, the injured person should be lying down with the head slightly lower than the trunk of the body and the legs elevated. Cover the wound with a thick, clean compress—such as sterile gauze, a handkerchief, or a towel—and apply steady pressure with the palm. (Direct pressure should not be used if a foreign object is embedded in the wound.) If blood soaks through the compress, do not remove it, but apply another compress over it and continue to exert pressure. While applying pressure, elevate the wound above the victim's heart. When bleeding stops, apply a bandage firmly enough to hold the compress in place but not so tightly as to cut off circulation.

If bleeding does not stop with direct pressure and elevation, the *pressure point technique* can be used. This method applies pressure to the artery that supplies blood to the wound by pressing it against the bone underneath (see illustration: Pressure Points). Apply firm pressure to the artery only until the bleeding stops. Seek medical assistance.

Internal Bleeding Traumatic injury, such as injury resulting from a fall or auto accident, may cause internal bleeding. Symptoms of internal bleeding include bleeding from the ears, nose, rectum, or vagina; vomiting or coughing up blood; and abdominal swelling or tenderness. As blood is lost and blood pressure drops sharply, the injured person may go into *shock*. Symptoms of shock include cool skin; shallow and rapid breathing; rapid and weak PULSE; trembling and restlessness; thirst; and feelings of weakness. (See also SHOCK, **3**.)

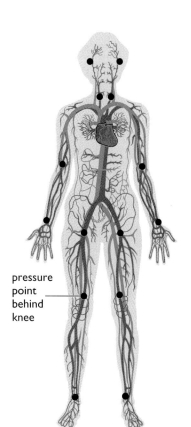

pressure point behind knee

Pressure Points. *The areas shown in the illustration are the approximate locations of arterial pressure points. Applying pressure to these areas cuts off arterial circulation to the area below the pressure point. Use pressure points only after trying direct pressure and elevation, and seek medical assistance immediately.*

CONSULT A
PHYSICIAN

First Aid for Internal Bleeding If internal bleeding is suspected, request immediate emergency medical assistance. Until help arrives, the victim should be kept warm and lying quietly and calmly with legs elevated. If the site of internal bleeding is known, a cold compress can be applied to the area. Do not give any food or liquids to someone who may be bleeding internally.

▶ # BODY TEMPERATURE

Body temperature is a measure of body heat. Normal body temperature for a healthy person is about 98.6°F (37°C) when measured with a thermometer placed under the tongue. A variation from normal temperature can be a sign of illness. Temperature fluctuations of plus or minus 1°F, however, can reflect normal changes in the body. For example, temperature varies during the day and is lowest early in the morning and highest late in the afternoon.

Taking Body Temperature You may use a mercury or digital thermometer to take body temperature. Before using a mercury thermometer, shake it sharply downward until it reads approximately 95°F (about 35°C). To take an *oral (sublingual) temperature,* place the thermometer under the tongue and leave it in place for at least 3 minutes before removing. (The person should not have had a hot or cold drink or a cigarette within a half hour and should hold the thermometer in place with the lips, not the teeth.) To read a mercury thermometer, hold it between thumb and first finger and, in good light, rotate the thermometer slowly until you see the line of mercury (see illustration: Reading a Thermometer). The closest marking to the end of the mercury is the body temperature. Digital thermometers provide a clear digital readout.

To take temperature under the *arm (subaxillary),* slip the thermometer into the armpit and leave it in place for at least 3 minutes before removing. Temperature can also be taken by placing a thermometer in a person's rectum. (A rectal thermometer with a short, stubby bulb should be used.) The bulb should be lubricated and inserted gently about 1 inch (about 2.5 cm). Leave in place for at least 2 minutes. A rectal temperature reading is the most accurate but tends to be about 1°F higher than the oral temperature. (See also FEVER, **2.**)

Reading a Thermometer. *To read a mercury thermometer, hold it between your thumb and forefinger and rotate it until you see the thin line of mercury. A normal oral temperature is 98.6°F, but temperatures of plus or minus 1°F are within a normal range.*

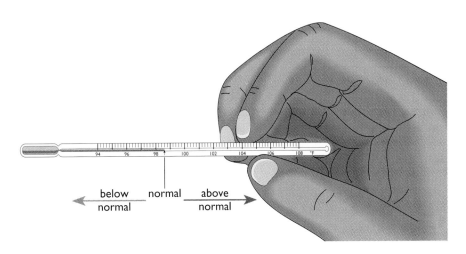

below normal ← normal → above normal

▷ BURNS

Burns are injuries that range from minor discomfort to life-threatening medical emergencies. They can be caused by fire, the sun, chemicals, hot objects or fluids, and ELECTRIC SHOCK. In the United States, 2 million people each year require medical treatment for burns. House fires cause the greatest number of deaths from burns. Children and the elderly are the most frequent victims of burns.

Classifying Burns The three categories of burns are based on the extent of damage to the skin: *First-degree burns* affect only the first, or outer, layer of the skin, causing redness, swelling, and pain. Most sunburns are an example of a first-degree burn. These burns heal quickly, and damaged skin usually peels away after the layer below heals. *Second-degree burns* affect the first and second layers of skin, causing blistering, intense redness, pain, and swelling. Deeper layers are left intact, and second-degree burns usually heal without scarring. *Third-degree burns* destroy both layers of the skin and may affect fat, nerves, muscles, and bones. The burned areas may look white or charred. Pain is often intense, but in the case of nerve damage there may be little or no pain.

First-degree burns can cause pain, restlessness, headache, and fever. Severe second-degree burns and third-degree burns result in loss of fluids from the burned area and can lead to *shock*. *Infection* is another serious complication from second- and third-degree burns, because the skin can no longer protect the body from bacteria.

First Aid for Burns Minor burns can be treated by holding the burned area under cool running water, immersing it in a cool-water bath, or applying cool-water compresses for at least 15 minutes. In the case of a chemical burn, flush the area with large quantities of cool running water. Jewelry should be removed before the area begins to swell.

Classifying Burns. *First-degree burns damage only the first, or outer, layer of skin. Second-degree burns damage the first and second layers. Third-degree burns destroy both layers and can also damage fat, nerves, muscles, and bone.*

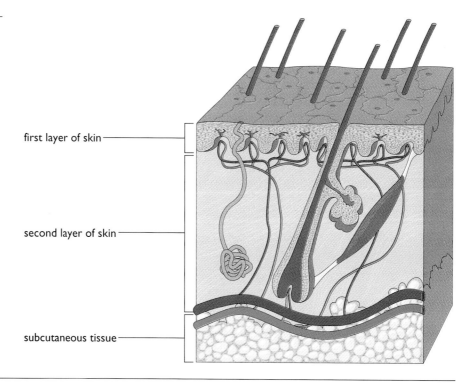

first layer of skin

second layer of skin

subcutaneous tissue

Cover the burn with sterile nonfluffy material or a clean cloth. Do not apply butter, oil, grease, or ointments to the area, and do not break the blisters.

To help a person with severe burns, first extinguish burning clothing, if necessary, by dousing the person with water or by rolling him or her in a blanket or coat on the ground. Make sure the heart is beating and the person is breathing; if these have stopped, CPR should be administered. Call for medical assistance immediately. Do not attempt to remove clothing that is stuck to a burn.

CONSULT A **PHYSICIAN**

Medical Treatment Second- and third-degree burns should be treated by a doctor, who may dress the burned area lightly with an antibacterial bandage or leave it exposed to promote healing. Analgesics may be given to relieve pain, and antibiotics may be prescribed if there are signs of infection. Shock is treated with intravenous fluids. Skin grafting may be done in patients with serious burns to minimize scarring. (See also FIRE SAFETY; SUN DAMAGE; SHOCK, 3.)

▶ CARBON DIOXIDE

Carbon dioxide (CO_2) is an odorless, colorless gas that is a natural component of the earth's atmosphere. A waste product of human and animal respiration, it can cause headaches, shortness of breath, and drowsiness when breathed in high concentrations. Trees and plants use carbon dioxide as part of the process of converting energy to food, called photosynthesis. Living plants thereby "recycle" carbon dioxide, returning their waste gas—oxygen—to the environment.

Carbon dioxide is also produced by the burning of such FOSSIL FUELS as coal, oil, gasoline, and natural gas. In the past century, huge increases in the use of fossil fuels have greatly added to the concentration of carbon dioxide in the atmosphere. Deforestation also makes carbon dioxide concentrations higher by eliminating oxygen-producing vegetation. Of special concern is the depletion of tropical forests such as those in South America's Amazon River basin. Many experts believe that these activities contribute to the health-threatening process of GLOBAL WARMING, in which an insulating layer of carbon dioxide and other gases traps heat in the lower atmosphere. (See also BIOSPHERE.)

▶ CARBON MONOXIDE POISONING

Carbon monoxide is a colorless, odorless, and extremely poisonous gas that is released by the burning of gasoline, oil, gas, wood, or coal in motor vehicle engines, furnaces, and stoves. It is a major contaminant in AIR POLLUTION. In the human body, carbon monoxide molecules prevent the hemoglobin in red blood cells from carrying oxygen to tissues, resulting in asphyxiation (suffocation). Prolonged exposure to carbon monoxide may cause brain damage, unconsciousness, and death.

Carbon monoxide poisoning can occur when an automobile engine is left running in a closed space like a garage or when a furnace malfunctions.

Furnace Inspection. *Furnaces should be inspected once a year to be sure they are clean and running properly. Improperly maintained furnaces can release dangerous levels of carbon monoxide.*

RISK FACTORS
▶ ▶ ▶ ▶ ▶ ▶

CONSULT A
PHYSICIAN

HEALTHY CHOICES
●●●●●●●●●●●●

Small quantities of carbon monoxide are also produced in cigarette smoke and by the pilot lights on gas stoves. Even small amounts of carbon monoxide can be deadly to persons suffering from emphysema or cardio-vascular disease.

Symptoms and Treatment Symptoms of carbon monoxide poisoning include dizziness, headaches, nausea, and faintness as well as flushed face and bright red lips. Because the gas is odorless, those in danger may be unaware that they are being poisoned. They may fall asleep, lapse into unconsciousness, and die. Treatment for people with carbon monoxide poisoning begins with taking them outdoors where they can get fresh air. If they are not breathing, someone trained in CPR (cardiopulmonary resuscitation) should begin *artificial respiration*. Emergency help should be summoned immediately.

Prevention To prevent carbon monoxide poisoning, never run a gasoline engine in a closed space. Make sure that all stoves and grills are properly vented, and never use an outdoor grill indoors. Have home furnaces inspected once a year to make sure they are clean and functioning properly.

▶ CARDIOPULMONARY RESUSCITATION see CPR

▶ CHILD ABUSE

Child abuse is any behavior that causes physical injury or emotional harm to a child. Child abuse is a serious social problem in the United States. Law enforcement and social service agencies estimate that as many as 2 million children are abused in some way each year and that between 4,000 and 5,000 children die from abuse each year. Child abuse also

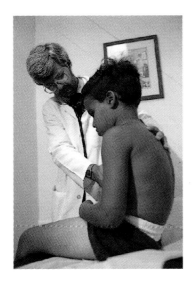

Treating Child Abuse. *A child who has been physically abused should be seen by a physician to determine the extent of the injuries and to begin treatment. Later, the child may be placed in a foster home to protect him or her from further abuse.*

RISK FACTORS
▶ ▶ ▶ ▶ ▶ ▶

CONSULT A
PHYSICIAN

causes lasting psychological damage. In most cases, the abusers of children are parents, stepparents, or other adults who are entrusted with caring for children.

Kinds of Abuse   Children may be abused in several ways. Many are the victims of physical VIOLENCE, such as being slapped, beaten, kicked, or burned. Infants and very young children can be severely injured or killed just by being shaken violently, which can cause blood vessels in the brain to rupture.

Not all forms of child abuse include physical violence. Some children are verbally or emotionally abused, which is still quite damaging. Name-calling and verbal humiliation can make children feel anxious, guilty, or worthless.

Another kind of abuse is *sexual abuse,* which can happen to both boys and girls. In sexual abuse, a parent or other authority figure takes advantage of a child's weakness and need for affection to obtain sexual gratification from the child. (See also SEXUAL ABUSE, **6.**)

Parental *neglect* is also a form of abuse. Some parents neglect their children by withholding the care, love, and stimulation they need. Babies with a condition called failure to thrive, meaning a failure to grow or develop normally, are often victims of neglect.

Causes of Child Abuse   Child abuse occurs in every socioeconomic class and among people of all races, religions, and educational levels. There are, however, some factors that appear to increase the risk of child abuse. Stress caused by poverty or unemployment, the abuse of alcohol or drugs, and a lack of social support systems can all trigger child abuse.

People who were themselves abused as children may repeat this behavior when they have a family. Becoming a parent at a very early age also increases the likelihood of an individual becoming abusive. Very young parents often lack the experience and parenting skills to cope with the demands of infants and small children, causing the parents to discipline or control children inappropriately.

Treating Child Abuse   Children who are at risk of being severely injured or killed need to be removed from the home immediately. After any injuries are treated, the children can be placed in foster care until the parents can receive counseling to prevent future abuse. Often abused children are identified by doctors, school nurses, or teachers who spot the evidence of physical abuse.

Many communities have social service agencies, such as a children and youth services department, that intervene when a child is being abused. Abusive parents or guardians can be charged with criminal offenses and imprisoned. They are usually required to undergo psychological counseling and parenting training. Parents can also seek help from special hot lines or support groups like Parents Anonymous. These organizations are available to help individuals deal with family problems.

An individual who sees or suspects child abuse should report the abuse immediately to a law enforcement or social service agency. An early report may save a child's life. More information or advice may be obtained by discussing the problem with a doctor, member of the clergy, or school official. In some communities, child abuse can be reported anonymously to the police or to a crisis hot line. (See also SPOUSE ABUSE.)

▷ CHILDPROOFING   see HOME SAFETY

▷ CHOKING

Universal Choking Sign. *The universal distress sign for choking is a hand on the throat with fingers and thumb extended.*

CONSULT A
PHYSICIAN

Choking occurs when food or a foreign object blocks a person's throat or windpipe, interrupting breathing. If the blockage is partial, the person can usually force the object out by coughing. If the airway is completely obstructed, the choking person will be unable to breathe and, unless treated promptly, will become unconscious and die of suffocation.

The main symptom of a choking emergency is the inability to speak. Other signs include gasping and struggling for breath and a bluish tinge to the skin. A choking person who cannot talk may clutch his or her neck in the universal choking sign (see illustration: Universal Choking Sign).

A choking emergency requires immediate first aid to clear the obstructed airway. There are several procedures, depending on the situation. An effective method for removing a morsel of food or other object blocking the windpipe is the HEIMLICH MANEUVER (abdominal thrust). Variations of this maneuver have been developed for use on unconscious victims, children, and infants. Another procedure is the *finger sweep,* which involves reaching a finger into the back of the choking person's throat to remove the obstruction. This procedure should be used only if the blockage can be seen. *Mouth-to-mouth resuscitation* may be necessary if the victim does not resume breathing after the obstruction is cleared. Emergency medical help should be called if the blockage cannot be cleared. (See also CPR.)

▷ CPR

CPR—*cardiopulmonary resuscitation*—is an emergency medical procedure used for reviving someone whose breathing and heart have stopped. Its purpose is to restore circulation of blood to the brain as quickly as possible to prevent brain damage and death. It is commonly used as a first aid treatment for victims of heart attacks, DROWNINGS, and serious ACCIDENTS. CPR should be used only if the victim's breathing and pulse have stopped. An emergency service should be called immediately.

CPR involves three main steps: opening and clearing the airway, restoring breathing, and restoring blood circulation. The order of these steps can be remembered by the letters **ABC** (Airway/Breathing/Circulation). After checking and opening the victim's *airway,* the person administering CPR alternately breathes into the victim's mouth (*mouth-to-mouth resuscitation*) and pushes on the sternum in a steady rhythm (*chest compressions*), simulating the effect of a heartbeat. Two people can perform CPR most efficiently: One breathes into the victim's mouth, and the other performs chest compressions.

Although it is easy to learn, performing CPR safely and effectively requires several hours of formal training, which is available to the public

Mouth-to-Mouth Resuscitation

(1) The rescuer clears the victim's airway of any obstructions.

(2) The rescuer opens the airway by tilting the victim's head backward slightly and raising the chin.

(3) The rescuer places his or her mouth tightly around the victim's mouth and blows one full breath into the victim's lungs. Then the rescuer takes a deep breath and blows a second full breath into the victim's lungs.

(4) The rescuer turns his or her head toward the victim's chest to listen for air being exhaled and to watch for the chest to fall.

Chest Compressions

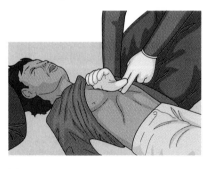

(5) The rescuer establishes proper hand position by measuring two finger widths above the bottom of the victim's sternum. The rescuer then places the heel of one hand in this location and interlocks the fingers of the other hand. The fingers cannot be allowed to rest on the ribs of the victim.

(6) The rescuer kneels over the victim and, with straight arms, pushes down rhythmically 15 times on the chest to a depth of 1 1/2 to 2 inches. The pushing is quick and firm, and the rescuer does not remove his or her hands from the victim's chest between compressions. After the count of 15, the rescuer checks breathing. Mouth-to-mouth resuscitation is performed again.

CPR. *CPR combines mouth-to-mouth resuscitation with chest compressions to open and clear the airway, restore breathing, and restore blood circulation. Mouth-to-mouth resuscitation involves four steps; chest compression involves two steps. Mouth-to-mouth resuscitation should be alternated with chest compressions until breathing is restored and a pulse can be felt.*

through the American Red Cross and American Heart Association. Special procedures can also be learned for performing CPR on infants and on young children. It is not recommended that CPR be attempted by people who have not received formal instruction unless there is no alternative. (See also EMERGENCY CARE SERVICES; FIRST AID; HEIMLICH MANEUVER.)

► DISLOCATIONS

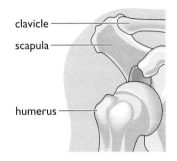

clavicle

scapula

humerus

Dislocated Shoulder Joint. *A dislocated shoulder joint is a common injury. When the shoulder is dislocated, the humerus is displaced from its normal position in the socket.*

A dislocation is an injury that occurs when the end of a bone is forced from its normal position in a joint. Usually caused by a blow or fall, a dislocation is characterized by deformity of the joint, swelling, and severe pain and may cause nerve damage or paralysis in some cases. Although most dislocations can be corrected by a physician, some require surgery.

The most common site for a dislocation is the shoulder, but the hips, spinal vertebrae, elbows, fingers, thumbs, and knees may also be affected. Occasionally babies are born with one or both hips dislocated. This condition requires early treatment to prevent permanent disability. Common in children is a dislocated elbow, which can occur when a child's arm is suddenly jerked by an adult.

In some cases, dislocations may result from an underlying disease, such as rheumatoid arthritis. Any dislocation can weaken the joint structure, making it more prone to subsequent dislocation.

The most obvious symptoms of a dislocation are loss of normal movement in the joint and severe pain. The affected joint swells and appears misshapen. If the condition is untreated, the unnatural movement of the bones may cause additional damage to the structure of the joint as well as to the surrounding muscles, ligaments, and blood vessels. Dislocation of the spinal vertebrae may result in damage to the spinal cord and paralysis.

CONSULT A PHYSICIAN

A person with no medical training should never attempt to return a dislocated bone to its correct position. Instead, the injured joint should be immobilized with a splint, pillow, or sling, and medical treatment should be sought immediately. A doctor will X-ray the joint to confirm the diagnosis and then carefully move, or *manipulate,* the bones back into position. If manipulation cannot be performed, the doctor will surgically reset them. Recurrent dislocation resulting from weak ligaments in a joint can also be remedied by surgery. Following treatment, the joint is immobilized with a cast or splint. (See also FRACTURES; SPRAINS AND STRAINS.)

► DROWNING

RISK FACTORS
► ► ► ► ► ►

Drowning is a fatal condition that occurs when a person is submerged in water or some other liquid long enough to suffocate. It is the third most common cause of accidental death in the United States; more than 7,000 deaths occur annually. Death by drowning is most frequent among children younger than the age of 5 and among people aged 15 to 25. Men are four times more likely to drown than women. Most drownings (50 to 75 percent) occur in lakes, rivers, and oceans, but many young children drown in swimming pools, especially pools without fencing. *Near-drownings* are nonfatal submersions in which oxygen deprivation is serious and sometimes causes injury or permanent brain damage.

Responding to Drowning Emergencies Only a strong swimmer well trained in water rescue should jump into the water to save a drowning person, because that person is liable to panic and drag the rescuer underwater. If the drowning person is floundering in water near a pier or side

Water Rescue. *Only a person who is well trained in life-saving techniques should jump into the water to save a person who is drowning.*

of a pool, someone who is not a strong swimmer can help by lying down and extending a hand, foot, pole, rope, towel, or other object. To help a drowning person who is far from shore, a rope or buoyant object can be thrown and used to pull him or her to shore, or a boat can be used to reach the person.

First Aid for Drowning As soon as possible, check for PULSE and breathing. If breathing has stopped, it is important to begin *mouth-to-mouth resuscitation* immediately and continue without interruption until the person is breathing regularly or until medical help arrives. It may be necessary to continue for several hours until the person's body has warmed and he or she begins breathing independently. Once normal breathing is established, keep the person warm, and seek medical attention. It is important to watch carefully to make sure that the person continues to breathe without interruption.

CONSULT A
PHYSICIAN

HEALTHY CHOICES

Measures to Prevent Drowning A few basic WATER SAFETY rules can help reduce drowning accidents: Never swim alone; don't jump into deep water without making sure there is an easy way to get out; wear a *life jacket* for all water sports; swim only in pools and beaches watched by lifeguards; never drink alcohol before swimming or participating in water sports; and never walk on ice-covered ponds or rivers unless it is certain the ice is safe. In addition, young children must be supervised at all times when they are swimming or taking a bath; childproof fencing must be installed around outdoor pools; and children should be taught to swim at an early age and taught that they must never swim without adult supervision. (See also CPR; HYPOTHERMIA.)

▶ **EARTHQUAKES** An earthquake is a motion of the earth's surface, caused by the sudden, rapid movement of the massive solid plates that lie under the oceans and continents. The intensity of an earthquake can range from a mild tremor to a violent motion capable of causing extensive damage over a

SAFETY AND ENVIRONMENTAL HEALTH

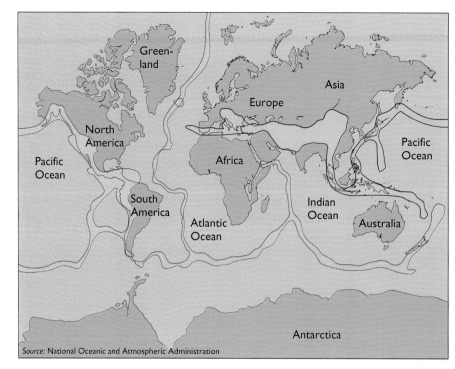

Earthquake-Prone Areas of the World. *Scientists keeping track of larger earthquakes over many years have defined several belts where quakes most often occur. These high-risk belts likely mark the boundaries of the massive plates that lie within the earth's crust.*

Source: National Oceanic and Atmospheric Administration

wide area. A million or so earthquakes occur every year, but most occur under the sea or are so mild that they are barely felt.

A large earthquake usually begins with a deep rumbling followed by violent movement of the ground. The tremors usually last only a few seconds, but they can cause buildings, bridges, and dams to collapse and large cracks to open in the ground. Earthquakes centered under the ocean may create huge tidal waves, which can cause flood and other damage in ocean-lying areas.

Most injuries or deaths in earthquakes are caused by falling bricks and plaster; splintering glass; toppling walls, furniture, or mirrors; fallen power lines; and fire. After a large quake, emergency services, sanitation systems, and utilities may be disrupted, which may lead to delayed medical treatment, contaminated food and water supplies, and the danger of explosion or fires.

RISK FACTORS
▶ ▶ ▶ ▶ ▶ ▶

HEALTHY CHOICES

Earthquake Preparedness Although earthquakes can strike in any region, certain parts of the world are at much higher risk for them (see illustration: Earthquake-Prone Areas of the World). In these areas especially, it is important to be prepared for an earthquake and to know how to react if one occurs. Preparedness includes bracing or bolting down large appliances and top-heavy objects in the home and keeping emergency supplies of food and water, a FIRST AID KIT, and a portable radio on hand. Governments in many high-risk areas have taken steps to reduce the potential for disaster by requiring new buildings to meet certain construction standards and by designing emergency plans for dealing with the aftermath of an earthquake.

HEALTHY CHOICES

Although the effects of an earthquake are unpredictable, people caught in one can take steps to reduce their chances of injury. People who are inside should stay inside, move away from windows, and seek shelter from potential falling objects in a hall or doorway or under a bed.

When the tremor is over, check the building for damage and fires, downed power lines, and gas leaks. Be prepared for additional tremors. People caught outside during an earthquake should stay away from power and telephone lines and structures that could fall. Try to move to an open area. (See also WEATHER-RELATED EMERGENCIES.)

▶ **ECOSYSTEM**

An ecosystem is a complex web of relationships among organisms and the nonliving elements in an area. Organisms include plants and animals as well as microorganisms like bacteria and fungi. The nonliving elements of an ecosystem include the air, water, and soil in the area.

The various elements of an ecosystem are interdependent, that is, each element depends on others to maintain the balance of the ecosystem. For example, sunlight and minerals from the soil help plants grow. Animals eat these plants, and, when the animals die, fungi help with the decomposition process, returning minerals to the soil. If even one small part of an ecosystem is destroyed, then the whole balance of the ecosystem may be destroyed also.

Ecosystems can be small or large. A pond and a decaying log are types of ecosystems. Islands, beaches, meadows, and forests are also ecosystems. The earth with its surrounding atmosphere is a vast ecosystem called the BIOSPHERE. Large ecosystems, such as deserts and tropical rain forests, in turn contain many smaller ecosystems.

Scientists are concerned about the impact of human activity on ecosystems. AIR POLLUTION and WATER POLLUTION, for example, can affect plant and animal life within a small ecosystem and upset the balance of nature there. Indeed, the balance of the biosphere itself may be endangered by human activity. For example, the destruction of tropical rain forests may be contributing to GLOBAL WARMING. And certain types of air pollution are thought to be depleting the OZONE layer, which acts as a shield to protect living things from the harmful effects of the sun's ultraviolet rays. Human health and the health of the planet as a whole may depend on understanding how ecosystems function and how humans can live within them without destroying their delicate balance. (See also ACID RAIN; AGRICULTURAL POLLUTION; THERMAL POLLUTION.)

How the Elements of an Ecosystem Interact. *The basic elements of an ecosystem might include (1) nonliving substances in the environment that provide energy and nutrients; (2) producers that manufacture food from nonliving substances; (3) consumers that eat other organisms; and (4) reducers that break down dead organisms and waste matter into substances that are used by producers.*

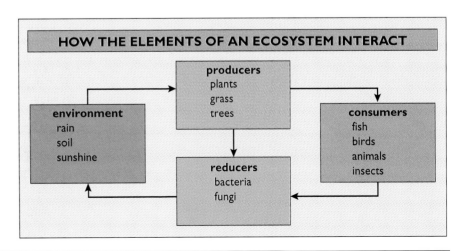

HOW THE ELEMENTS OF AN ECOSYSTEM INTERACT

producers
plants
grass
trees

environment
rain
soil
sunshine

consumers
fish
birds
animals
insects

reducers
bacteria
fungi

▷ ELECTRICAL SAFETY

Electrical safety involves taking precautions that can help prevent shocks, INJURIES, and deaths caused by electricity and electrical tools and appliances. Most ACCIDENTS involving electricity are caused by improper use of electrical appliances and problems with plugs, outlets, and extension cords. Each year in the United States, about 46,000 fires are caused by faults in home electrical systems. The following safety guidelines can help prevent electrical accidents.

Ground Fault Circuit Interrupter. *It is important to keep electrical appliances away from tubs and sinks. However, this electronic device, also called a GFCI, shuts off the current under certain circumstances in which a potentially lethal shock could be delivered.*

Safe Use of Electrical Equipment Here are a few tips for using electrical equipment safely:

- Grasp the plug, not the cord, when unplugging an appliance or tool from an outlet.
- Use grounded three-pronged outlets for three-pronged plugs.
- Avoid overloading an outlet with too many plugs.
- Use extension cords only as a short-term measure. When you need an extension cord, use one of the correct wire size. Never string a series of cords together. Keep extension cords out of traffic areas, and never run them under rugs or carpeting.
- Unplug small appliances and put them away when they are not in use.
- Electric blankets are common fire hazards. Follow directions for their use. For example, do not fold or crease electric blankets, and never use them to dry damp bedding or on a bed where bed-wetting may occur.

Maintaining Electrical Equipment Keeping electrical equipment in good repair involves the following:

- Replace worn, frayed cords and worn plugs. Check appliances frequently for problems.
- If you feel even a slight shock while using an appliance, turn off the power and carefully unplug the equipment. Use it again only when the cause of the problem has been identified and repaired.

Special Care Near Water Water is an excellent conductor of electricity and can transmit severe shocks. Special precautions are needed:

- Avoid using any electrical device in a damp area or near water. If the appliance falls into the water, a fatal electric shock could result. For this reason keep small electrical appliances away from tubs and sinks.
- Disconnect electric power in the event of a flood in a house or basement because electric current may be traveling through the water.
- Make sure your hands are dry when using electrical equipment.
- Take special care when cleaning electrical equipment. Always unplug the appliance first.

Safety Devices Safety devices in your home can prevent many electrical accidents:

HEALTHY CHOICES

- Install electronic devices called ground fault circuit interrupters (GFCIs) that can prevent severe or fatal shocks by shutting off

HEALTHY CHOICES

the current in dangerous situations. If a hair dryer should fall into the bathtub, for example, the GFCI will shut off the current. An electrician can install these devices in bathroom or kitchen outlets or in circuit breakers without any rewiring. Portable GFCI devices that plug into any receptacle are available at hardware and building supply stores.

▸ When young children are in the home, cover unused outlets with plastic safety covers so that they cannot stick their fingers or metal objects into the outlets. (See also BURNS; ELECTRIC SHOCK; FIRE SAFETY; HOME SAFETY.)

▶ ELECTRIC SHOCK

Electric shock is caused by an electric current entering and leaving the body. Even small currents are capable of knocking a person down or unconscious, stopping both breathing and heartbeat, and causing death. In the United States, more than 1,000 people die every year from electrical accidents, and the electric shock of lightning kills an additional 300.

RISK FACTORS
▶ ▶ ▶ ▶ ▶ ▶

The human body, especially when wet, is a good conductor of electricity. Moist skin allows greater amounts of electrical current to enter underlying tissues, where it can cause widespread damage including severe burns. Thus, a person in a bathtub of water may be killed by a shock that a person in a dry environment would survive.

First Aid for Electric Shock Do not attempt first aid until contact with the electrical current has been broken (see illustration: First Aid for Electric Shock). Switch off the current if possible, or remove the person from the source of electricity using nonconducting material such as a wooden chair or broomstick or a dry rope. Check breathing and heart rate. If the person is breathing but unconscious, provide FIRST AID for visible BURNS and summon medical help. If no breathing is detected, begin *mouth-to-mouth resuscitation;* if no heartbeat is detected, begin CPR immediately. (See also ELECTRICAL SAFETY.)

CONSULT A
PHYSICIAN

First Aid for Electric Shock.
Do not touch a person who has been shocked until the current has been broken. Either switch off the current or use a nonconducting material such as a wooden chair or broomstick or a dry rope to separate the person from the source of electricity.

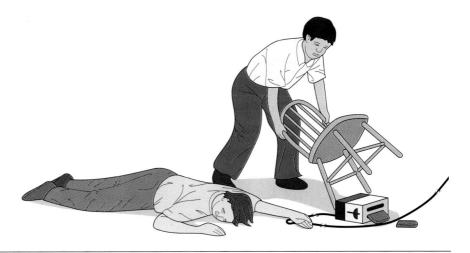

► EMERGENCY CARE SERVICES

Emergency care services provide immediate medical care to people suffering from serious or life-threatening medical conditions. They include rescue squads, emergency ambulance services, paramedics, hospital emergency rooms, burn centers, and trauma centers. Emergency care services typically treat an extremely wide range of conditions, including heart attacks, serious burns, broken bones, head injuries, BITES AND STINGS, severe allergy attacks, drug overdoses, POISONING, uncontrolled BLEEDING, gunshot and stab WOUNDS, convulsions, and CHOKING.

Most rescue squads and emergency ambulance services are staffed by *emergency medical technicians* (EMTs), trained personnel who can perform emergency medical procedures like CPR and administer medication on the way to the hospital. Some rescue squads, however, are operated by personnel who can only provide transportation to the hospital.

An ambulance or rescue squad service should be summoned if a person is unconscious, choking, or bleeding profusely; having convulsions, difficulty breathing, or chest pains; or suffering from HYPOTHERMIA, a high fever, or some other severe medical condition. An emergency service should not be called in nonemergency situations.

Hospital emergency rooms have become major providers of nonemergency health care, because they are open most hours of the day. In most hospital emergency rooms, nurses evaluate incoming patients to distinguish between serious or life-threatening conditions, such as heart attacks, and people with nonemergency conditions, who can wait to be seen.

People who have been badly injured or burned in accidents may be taken to a trauma center or burn center. A *trauma center* is a specially equipped emergency room where medical specialists treat severe injuries and perform emergency surgery. Badly burned patients are usually transferred to *burn centers* where the staff uses state-of-the-art equipment and techniques to save lives and minimize scarring.

Emergency Services. *A paramedic can provide life-saving treatments and medications while in the ambulance on the way to the hospital.*

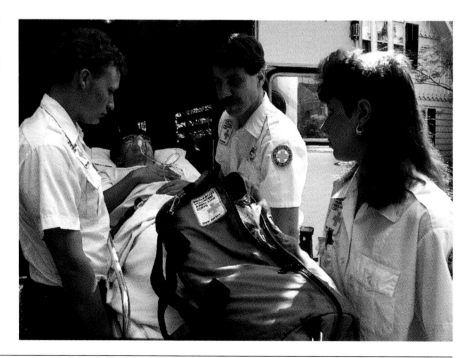

Another kind of emergency medical facility is the *emergency care center.* These privately owned emergency clinics function like hospital emergency rooms but are not attached to hospitals. People with minor health problems that require immediate attention, such as a sprain, acute infection, dog bite, or cut requiring stitches, typically use emergency care centers.

It is a good idea to investigate the emergency care facilities in your area and choose in advance the ambulance service and emergency room to call in the event of a serious illness or accident. The emergency room should be close by, and it should have a good reputation. It is important to know the hours of the day that the various emergency facilities in the area are staffed by physicians. The hours and a list of the telephone numbers for emergency services should be kept near all telephones. It is also a good idea to know ahead of time how the facility expects payment. (See also FIRST AID; INJURIES; POISON-CONTROL CENTERS; EMERGENCY MEDICAL TECHNICIAN, **9**; HOSPITAL, **9**.)

▶ **EMERGENCY MEDICAL IDENTIFICATION**   Emergency medical identification should be carried by people who have certain serious medical conditions. Conveyed on special bracelets, necklaces, or cards, this information alerts rescue personnel and doctors to conditions such as diabetes, epilepsy, hemophilia, glaucoma, heart condition, and allergy to particular medications, such as penicillin.

Medic Alert Tags. *Some people with serious medical conditions should wear medical identification tags in case of an emergency.*

These bracelets, necklaces, and cards are sold in drugstores and pharmacies and through doctors and hospitals. All carry the *universal medical emergency identification symbol* and provide space to specify the wearer's name, address, telephone number, medical condition, and medication, if any. For patients who have lost consciousness or the ability to speak, emergency medical identification can be critical to their chances of survival and full recovery from illness or injury.

▶ **EMERGENCY PROCEDURES**   see FIRST AID

▶ **ENERGY CONSERVATION**   Energy conservation involves reducing the amount of electricity, fossil fuels, and other power sources used for such purposes as heating and lighting buildings, powering vehicles, and running factories. Individuals can conserve energy by changing their habits and activities to use less energy, while industries can aid conservation by using more energy-efficient machinery.

Benefits of Energy Conservation   Using less energy conserves limited natural resources, including FOSSIL FUELS such as oil, natural gas, and coal. It can reduce the AIR POLLUTION that is often a by-product of energy

---

TIPS FOR ENERGY CONSERVATION

Use carpools, public transportation, and bicycles.

Drive a uniform 55 mph (88 kph) on highways.

Keep automobile engine in tune.

Keep tires properly inflated.

Turn off the engine if automobile will be stopped for more than 1 minute.

Set thermostat at 68°F (20°C) in the winter and 78°F (26°C) in the summer.

Close flue when fireplace is not in use.

Turn off lights when not needed.

Use fluorescent light bulbs in place of incandescent bulbs.

Use dishwasher, washer, and dryer only when loads are full.

Clean air conditioner filters monthly.

Clean condenser coils on back of refrigerator yearly.

Defrost refrigerator before frost builds up to more than 1/4 inch.

Set refrigerator at 38° to 42°F (3.3° to 5.5°C) and freezer at 0° to 5°F (−17.7° to −14.9°C).

---

use. In recent years, scientists have advised using fewer fossil fuels in order to slow GLOBAL WARMING. CARBON DIOXIDE emissions, created when fossil fuels are burned, are believed to contribute to global warming. Another benefit of conserving energy is that it saves money. This money can be spent in other ways, even to develop further energy-conservation measures.

HEALTHY CHOICES

Conserving Energy   There are a number of ways that individuals and groups can eliminate waste and conserve energy. Installing adequate insulation and storm windows can greatly reduce the amount of energy required to heat and cool the average home each year. Home heating furnaces should be cleaned and checked yearly to make sure they are operating at maximum efficiency. Using a heat pump, a device that uses heat energy in the atmosphere for heating and cooling, can reduce the energy needed to heat a home by up to 40 percent. Keeping the thermostat at 68°F (20°C) in winter and 78°F (26°C) in summer can also greatly reduce electrical and fuel use. Another way to conserve energy is to use fluorescent light bulbs in lamps. Fluorescent bulbs are more expensive to buy, but they last longer and use less energy than ordinary light bulbs.

Car pools, buses, and trains are energy-efficient ways to commute to work or school. Public transportation carries more people, uses less energy, and produces fewer pollutants than private automobiles. Walking or riding a bicycle whenever possible saves energy and also provides exercise.

Governments can promote energy conservation as well. They can levy high taxes on fossil fuels and encourage the development of convenient public transportation systems. Our national, state, and local governments now require the production of more energy-efficient cars, encourage better home insulation, and promote the recycling of waste products such as aluminum, glass, and newspaper. Clean air and water laws help reduce pollution and foster more efficiency in industry. (See also SOLAR ENERGY.)

▷ ENVIRONMENTAL ORGANIZATIONS

Environmental organizations are groups dedicated to the management and/or conservation and preservation of natural resources. Some organizations are government agencies responsible for such things as developing environmental protection policies, establishing pollution standards, and enforcing environmental regulations in business. Other organizations are private groups that work to change governmental and industrial policies that threaten the environment and promote public awareness of environmental issues.

Governmental Groups The main groups within the U.S. government concerned with environmental issues are the Department of the Interior, the Department of Energy, the Environmental Protection Agency (EPA), and the Forest Service, which is an agency within the Department of Agriculture. The *Department of the Interior* is the main U.S. conservation agency. It administers most federal land and is responsible for both the conservation and the development of water, mineral, and wildlife resources. It also manages the nation's parks and historic areas. The *Department of Energy* is responsible for developing and coordinating national energy policies. It promotes conservation of fuel and electricity and regulates interstate power companies. The Department of Energy also conducts research to develop new energy sources and more efficient energy use. The *Environmental Protection Agency* has responsibility for protecting the nation's environment from pollution. It establishes and enforces environmental protection standards and conducts research on the effects of pollution. The *Forest Service* promotes the best use of the nation's forests, which includes protecting forests against insects, disease, and fire; preserving wildlife; and managing timber resources.

Nongovernmental Groups There are a number of nongovernmental environmental organizations. Their efforts have often played a significant role in protecting threatened ECOSYSTEMS and endangered species. Some are concerned with a variety of environmental issues, whereas others are more focused on a particular issue, such as wildlife preservation.

The *Sierra Club* is one of the best-known American environmental organizations. The Sierra Club organizes conferences, lectures, films, exhibits, and various types of outdoor expeditions through local groups throughout the country. The club also sponsors committees devoted to saving threatened scenic areas and wildlife. *Greenpeace,* begun in Canada, is an international environmental organization that works to halt practices and policies that threaten the environment. The group is best known for its methods of protest, which involve interfering directly but nonviolently with such activities as whaling, offshore oil drilling, and the testing of nuclear weapons at sea. *Worldwatch Institute* focuses primarily on informing policymakers and the public about the links between the world economy and the environment. Its aim is to raise international awareness of such issues as GLOBAL WARMING, OZONE depletion, world water shortages, and soil erosion so that governments will take action to address the problems. Although these groups are among the best known, there are a host of other environmental organizations, including the National Aubudon Society, the Nature Conservancy, the Wilderness Society, and the World Wildlife Fund.

> The efforts of nongovernmental environmental organizations have often played a significant role in protecting threatened ecosystems and endangered species.

▶ FIRE SAFETY

Fire safety involves precautions, procedures, and equipment that can help prevent INJURIES and deaths caused by fire. In the United States, more than 3 million fires are reported each year. Fires injure more than 28,000 people and cause about 4,400 deaths annually. Fire safety includes knowing how to prevent fires from happening and what to do if a fire occurs.

Preventing Fires   Fires can occur anywhere, but in homes the most common places for fires to start are the living room, kitchen, garage, basement, and bedroom. These rooms are likely to contain combustible items or electrical equipment that could start a fire. Fire prevention involves not only reducing the probability of fire but being prepared to deal quickly with any fire that might start. The following are important means of fire prevention:

HEALTHY CHOICES

- ▸ Store flammable materials carefully. Gasoline, paint, and flammable cleaning fluids should be stored in tightly closed cans away from heat or flame. Oily rags can burst into flame spontaneously and should be discarded. Keeping storage areas clear of papers and fabrics is important. Some communities have special cleanup weeks when homeowners and businesses can discard trash and eliminate fire hazards.
- ▸ Be careful in the kitchen. Grease and oil are highly flammable and must be kept from flames and heat sources.
- ▸ Use caution with fireplaces and stoves. Use protective screens with fireplaces, and clean flues regularly so that flammable tars do not accumulate. Coal stoves, wood stoves, and portable heaters should be used with care and never left unattended. A fire extinguisher should be kept near all fireplaces, stoves, and portable heaters.

Fire Extinguishers. *The label of a fire extinguisher will tell what kinds of fires it will put out. "All class" fire extinguishers put out all kinds of fires.*

- Take care with cigarettes—they are a very common cause of house fires. Provide ashtrays for smokers, and make sure cigarettes are completely extinguished. A smoker should never smoke in bed or when sleepy.
- Special protection is needed for children. Matches should be placed out of children's reach, and parents should teach children never to play with matches. Parents can buy sleepwear for children made of fire-resistant materials.
- Keep all electrical equipment in good repair. Check household wiring periodically for worn, frayed cords. Use extension cords only as a short-term measure, and avoid overloading outlets. (See also ELECTRICAL SAFETY.)
- Install and maintain fire safety devices. Inexpensive home devices can help put out small fires and reduce injuries and deaths from larger ones. Keep fire extinguishers on hand in the kitchen, garage, and basement as well as near stairways. All adults should know how to use them. Install smoke detectors on every floor, and test them regularly.

If a Fire Starts If a fire starts, it is vital to know what to do to prevent injury and death. Following are some helpful tips:

HEALTHY CHOICES

- If a fire is small, it may be possible to put it out with a fire extinguisher. It is important to use the right type of extinguisher. "All class" extinguishers can be used for any type of fire; "class B" extinguishers can be used for grease fires; and "class C" extinguishers can be used for electrical fires. Grease fires in pans may be put out by covering the pan with a lid. When using an extinguisher, stay back, and spray the nozzle at the base of the flames.
- Hold periodic household fire drills so that everyone will know what to do if a fire starts. Plan escape routes ahead of time, and make sure an adult is responsible for every child. For upper-story bedrooms, install fire ladders or other means of escape.
- Leave a burning building quickly. Call for help from a neighboring building, and never return to the house to rescue pets or possessions. Family members can meet at a prearranged place to be sure all are safe.
- Leave safely. Never open a door that feels hot; use another escape route. If you do get trapped in a room by fire, shut the door and block any cracks with blankets or other material to keep smoke from entering the room. Go to a window and shout for help. If smoke has filled the room, you may need to lean out the window for fresh air. When moving through a smoke-filled area, stay close to the floor where smoke is less dense.
- If clothing catches on fire, drop to the ground immediately and roll to smother the flames. If possible, wrap up in a nearby rug or blanket. Clothing fires can cause serious BURNS.

Knowing how to prevent fires and how to act safely if a fire starts are important ways to protect your life and your home. Most local fire departments will provide individuals with free fire safety information. (See also HOME SAFETY; SMOKE INHALATION.)

▷ FIRST AID

First aid is providing immediate care in the event of illness or injury. The purpose of emergency first aid is to prevent the injury from becoming worse, to maintain vital functions, and to reassure the patient and make him or her comfortable while waiting for medical assistance. In life-threatening situations such as heart attack, choking, extensive bleeding, or shock, emergency first aid can save lives. A basic rule is to remain calm and evaluate the situation before attempting any treatment.

Minor Injuries   First aid for minor INJURIES typically involves treating uncomplicated cuts, bruises, BURNS, and SPRAINS AND STRAINS. Every home should have a well-stocked medicine cabinet or FIRST AID KIT so that supplies are on hand to treat an injury. The kit should include an assortment of bandages, gauze pads and wraps, and aspirin or an aspirin substitute. Syrup of ipecac and activated charcoal should also be included if there are small children in the house.

HEALTHY CHOICES

Medical Emergencies   Learning basic first aid emergency procedures—such as administering CPR (cardiopulmonary resuscitation), controlling bleeding, and treating shock—will help you deal with medical emergencies. The first priority is to evaluate the situation and provide immediate life-saving treatment when necessary. Help should be summoned, but the victim should never be left alone. A seriously injured person must be transported to the nearest hospital or trauma center as soon as possible. If you call 911 or other EMERGENCY CARE SERVICES, you will need to provide certain information—your location, telephone number, name, the nature of the emergency, and a brief description of what happened. Do not hang up the telephone until the operator ends the conversation.

Emergency First Aid   The first step is to check consciousness by gently tapping the person and asking if he or she is okay. Next, check breathing: Listen to the victim's chest, and look for it to rise and fall. Third, take a PULSE at the artery in the neck. If the victim is not breathing but has a pulse, *mouth-to-mouth resuscitation* should be started immediately. If there is no heartbeat, CPR should be administered. These procedures should be attempted only by people who are trained to perform them.

Treating Shock. *If an injured person shows signs of shock, keep the person lying down, make sure that the person is warm enough, and elevate the legs (unless neck or back injuries are suspected).*

WHAT TO DO IN AN EMERGENCY

Immediate treatment

Call out for someone to get help.

Look, listen, and feel for breathing.

Determine if the victim's heart is beating.

Stop excessive bleeding.

If something has been swallowed, ask victim what it was.

Treat for shock.

Perform the Heimlich maneuver for choking.

What to tell doctor or paramedics

What has happened.

What the victim's noticeable injuries, symptoms, or signs are.

When the accident occurred or symptoms or signs began.

If known, what medications the victim has taken.

If poisoning has occurred, what has been swallowed, and when.

Where you and/or the victim are.

The phone number of your location.

Ask what more you can do to help.

Source: The American Medical Association. *Handbook of first aid and emergency care.*

Heavy BLEEDING can quickly cause death and must be controlled immediately. This is done by applying direct pressure to an open wound with a clean cloth or hand (it is important to wear gloves whenever possible when providing first aid to someone who is bleeding to prevent the spread of infection). Elevating the wound will also help slow bleeding.

If the victim's breathing is shallow and pulse is rapid and weak, the victim may be in *shock,* a condition in which normal blood flow is impaired. Treatment for shock involves keeping the victim lying down, making sure that he or she does not lose body heat, and elevating the legs to improve blood circulation. (See also SHOCK, 3.)

CHOKING requires immediate action. In most cases, this means performing the HEIMLICH MANEUVER, a technique of putting pressure on the victim's abdomen to dislodge the foreign object.

Courses in basic first aid techniques are usually taught at local branches of the American Red Cross, YMCA, YWCA, American Heart Association, and in school and community centers. (See also ACCIDENTS; DROWNING; FRACTURES; POISONING; MEDICINE CABINET, 7; EMERGENCY MEDICAL TECHNICIAN, 9.)

▶ **FIRST AID KIT**   A first aid kit consists of emergency medical supplies for treating injuries and illnesses. It should be standard equipment in every home, workplace, car, and boat; hikers and campers should carry a portable first aid kit among their supplies.

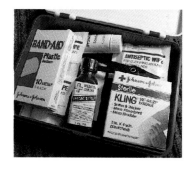

First Aid Supplies. *Every home, car, and boat should have a well-stocked first aid kit.*

A typical first aid kit includes an assortment of gauze pads and wraps, elastic bandages for wrapping sprained joints, large triangular bandages to use as slings, and adhesive tape. The kit should also contain a fever thermometer, scissors, tweezers, and safety pins, in addition to basic medications, such as aspirin and an aspirin substitute, syrup of ipecac (to induce vomiting), an antiseptic cream, ointment, or spray, and hydrogen peroxide for cleaning wounds. A flashlight, flares, and a blanket should be included in first aid kits for boats and cars. Hikers and campers should also carry calamine lotion, corticosteroid cream and antihistamine (to relieve itchy rashes), a snakebite kit, a foil (or "space") blanket, and medicine to control diarrhea.

People with special medical conditions need to keep additional supplies in their first aid kits. People with diabetes should stock an extra supply of insulin and a candy bar or other simple sugar to prevent diabetic shock, and people who are allergic to insect stings should include an adrenaline syringe in their kits. All first aid kits should be checked from time to time, and any missing supplies or expired medications should be replaced. (See also FIRST AID.)

FOSSIL FUELS

Fossil fuels are naturally occurring materials used to produce heat or power that have been formed from the remains of prehistoric organisms. Fossil fuels such as coal, oil, and natural gas are essential to modern life. However, all fossil fuels contain *hydrocarbons,* chemical compounds made up of hydrogen and carbon that can be poisonous. The burning of fossil fuels has led to ACID RAIN and AIR POLLUTION. Also, many experts believe that the gases released from burning these fuels contribute to GLOBAL WARMING. All of these environmental consequences have negative impacts on human health.

Uses and Dangers of Fossil Fuels Fossil fuels are the primary source of energy throughout the world. *Coal* is mainly used to produce electricity, to heat buildings, and to provide energy for industrial machinery. The most plentiful fossil fuel, it may also be the most environmentally damaging. In addition to its role in causing air pollution and contributing to global warming, the use of coal in industry and in generating electricity is responsible for acid rain that damages crops, forests, and lakes.

Crude oil, or *petroleum,* is one of the most valuable fossil fuels. When refined into heating oil, diesel fuel, and gasoline, it is used for home and industrial heating and for powering the engines of automobiles and other machines. Because of its widespread use in automobile fuel, oil is one of the primary contributors to both air pollution and global warming. Oil has also been the source of many ecological disasters as a result of OIL SPILLS from tankers, pipelines, and drilling rigs.

Natural gas, used for heating, cooking, and providing energy for industry, is the least damaging of the fossil fuels because its combustion produces fewer harmful substances than coal or oil.

Cutting Down on Fossil Fuels In response to rising environmental and health concerns, many experts have called for reductions in the use

Automobile Emissions. *Gasoline is a refined fossil fuel. Automobile emissions create harmful air pollution and may also contribute to global warming.*

of fossil fuels. Already, clean-air laws in the United States have led to decreased use of coal and to the increased use of devices to try to prevent the release of pollutants into the atmosphere. Many experts believe, however, that the solution lies in the development of greater energy efficiency and on the increased use of cleaner, alternative sources of energy. Technologies such as wind power, geothermal energy, and SOLAR ENERGY are possible alternatives. These energy sources are not only cleaner, but they are also renewable, unlike fossil fuels. Individuals can practice ENERGY CONSERVATION to reduce the demand for fossil fuels. (See also CARBON DIOXIDE.)

▶ FRACTURES

A fracture is a break in a bone. Fractures occur most frequently in the bones of the arms and legs and can be caused by a fall, a blow, or some other INJURY. Most fractures are caused by injuries that exert extreme force on a bone. In addition, certain diseases, like osteoporosis and some types of cancer, weaken bones so that they can break in a minor injury.

RISK FACTORS
▶ ▶ ▶ ▶ ▶ ▶

Elderly people are especially prone to fractures because their bones have become fragile and also because they tend to fall more often than younger adults. (See also OSTEOPOROSIS, 3.)

Types of Fractures There are two main types of fractures. In a *closed (or simple) fracture,* the broken ends of the bone remain under the skin and there is little or no damage to the surface tissue. An *open (or compound) fracture* includes an open wound that is associated with the break in the bone. In severe open fractures, bone ends may poke through the skin. Open fractures carry a great danger of infection and shock. Fractures may also be categorized according to the pattern of the break (see illustration: Common Fractures).

Common Fractures. *Common types of fractures include:* (a) transverse, *in which the bone is broken straight across;* (b) oblique, *in which the break is diagonal; and* (c) greenstick, *in which the bone does not break all the way through. This type of fracture is common among children.*

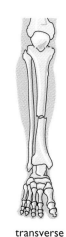
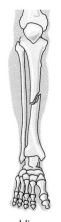
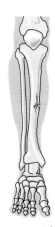

transverse   oblique   greenstick

First Aid for Fractures   The site of a fracture is often swollen, discolored, and tender. Pain in the area may be severe and made worse by movement. There may be loss of function in the area of injury and deformity of the affected limb. In a compound fracture, bone may protrude through an open wound in the skin. Broken bones may also cause internal injury or bleeding, especially when the ribs or pelvis are broken. (See also FIRST AID.)

CONSULT A
PHYSICIAN

A person with a suspected fracture should be given medical care, and medical assistance should be called to immobilize the suspected fracture during transfer to the hospital. A person with a spinal fracture should not be moved unless his or her life is in immediate danger. Specific types of first aid should be administered to protect the body from further damage.

No attempt should be made to set or straighten a broken bone; instead, it should be splinted as is with as little movement as possible. *Splinting* involves immobilizing a limb temporarily to prevent further injury. Splinting is usually done by tying the limb to something rigid such as a board or stick. The splint should be padded (with newspapers, towels, blanket) before it is placed against the fractured limb, and the attachment should be snug but not tight enough to cut off circulation. Open wounds should be covered with a sterile dressing. Severe BLEEDING needs to be treated immediately with appropriate first aid procedures.

Medical Treatment   A physician who suspects a fracture will have X rays taken to provide a clear picture of the bone. The X ray will show if a fracture has occurred and, if so, the type and extent of the fracture. (See also X-RAY EXAMINATION, **3.**)

When there is a fracture, the physician realigns the bone ends in their normal anatomical position so that the bone will heal without deformity. Then the bone is immobilized, in most cases by a plaster or fiberglass cast. If the fracture is unstable, metal screws, pins, plates, or wires may be used to keep the bone pieces aligned.

Recovery Process   Bones begin to heal immediately after a fracture. Blood clots form at the bone ends, stopping bleeding, and the immune system gears up to fight infection. In time, new tissue forms that eventually develops into dense, strong bone. Recovery time varies considerably depending on the age of the individual and the location and severity of the break. Babies and children heal more easily and quickly than adults, for whom complete recovery may take 6 months or more. (See also ACCIDENTS; DISLOCATIONS.)

▶ FROSTBITE

Frostbite, freezing of parts of the body, is caused by exposure to very cold temperatures. It most often affects extremities such as the toes, fingers, nose, and ears. Frostbite occurs when parts of the body freeze and ice crystals form in the cell fluid. As the freezing progresses, normal functions stop, and cells begin to die.

Symptoms and Complications   The first symptoms of frostbite are cold, painful, and reddened skin. As frostbite develops, the pain eases and patches of skin turn white or gray. In later stages, the skin may look blue and blisters may form. Severe frostbite may cause *gangrene*, in which the tissues die. (See also GANGRENE, **3.**)

Frostbite First Aid   To care for minor frostbite outdoors, cover the frostbitten part of the body with extra clothing or a warm cloth. Put frostbitten fingers or hands under the armpit for extra warmth. Never massage the frostbitten area or rub it with snow. It is important to bring a person with frostbite inside as soon as possible. The frostbitten area should be placed in warm water, between 100 and 104°F (between 38 and 40°C), for 45 minutes to 1 hour. Gentle exercise may also help speed rewarming. Do not expose the skin to intense heat or apply ointment. As soon as the skin becomes pink or the feeling begins to return, stop the warming process. Apply a dry cloth between fingers and toes, and seek medical attention immediately to evaluate the extent of tissue damage.

CONSULT A
PHYSICIAN

HEALTHY CHOICES
● ● ● ● ● ● ● ● ● ● ● ●

Preventing Frostbite   Warm clothing, especially on the head, face, hands, and feet, is the best protection against frostbite during cold-weather activities. Always be aware of the wind-chill factor, and take regular breaks to come inside to warm up. (See also HYPOTHERMIA.)

Frostbite.   *Frostbite is a constant concern for those who spend long periods of time exposed to very cold weather.*

▷ **GENETIC ENGINEERING**   Genetic engineering is the application of laboratory techniques to manipulate or alter the genes, or hereditary material, of an organism. By altering an organism's genes, scientists can change particular characteristics of the organism. This makes it possible to correct certain genetic defects, improve genetic characteristics, or even create new life forms.

Gene Splicing   The main technique used in genetic engineering is gene splicing (also called recombinant-DNA formation), in which genetic material from one organism is transferred to another. The genes of an organism are carried on the long coils of *DNA* (deoxyribonucleic acid) molecules. Scientists use special enzymes to break a DNA strand. A gene-sized fragment of DNA from another organism is then spliced (joined) into the break. The newly combined strand, called *recombinant DNA*, is reinserted into a cell, where it reproduces itself each time the cell divides.

Applications of Genetic Engineering   Two of the main areas of use are in medicine and food production. In medicine, genetic engineering has made it possible to mass produce certain hormones, such as insulin and human growth hormone, as well as the protein interferon, which is being tested for use against viruses and other diseases. Genetic engineering has also been used to develop several new drugs, vaccines, and other medically important substances.

A promising use of genetic engineering in human cells is *gene therapy*, which may provide a cure for certain diseases. Many inherited diseases are caused by the failure of a particular gene to perform its function, such as to produce a needed hormone or enzyme. In gene therapy, physicians remove cells from an ill person, genetically alter them to correct the defect, and then return the modified cells to the patient's body, where they produce the missing substance. A person with hemophilia, for instance, can be given genes that enable him or her to produce the lacking blood-clotting factor. Although still in its infancy, gene therapy offers hope for people with inherited disorders like cystic fibrosis and sickle cell anemia and may also help treat AIDS and cancer.

Among the uses of genetic engineering in agriculture is the altering of foods to improve such qualities as flavor, nutritional value, disease resistance, and shelf life. Several varieties of fruits, vegetables, and grains have already been developed, including, for example, a tomato containing an extra gene that prevents it from rotting too quickly. Other areas of research and development are genetically altered livestock, such as fish and poultry, and genetically engineered pesticides.

Problems and Questions   The use of genetic engineering has raised several potential problems and concerns. One concern involves safety. Some medical researchers fear that implanting genetically altered cells in humans might result in unplanned effects, such as an increased risk of cancers or other diseases. Critics of genetically engineered foods are concerned that they pose new safety risks and believe new foods should be thoroughly tested before going to market and clearly labeled for the consumer. In 1992, the U.S. Food and Drug Administration determined that genetically altered food poses little risk and would not generally be subject to testing and regulation.

> Although still in its infancy, gene therapy offers hope for people with inherited disorders like cystic fibrosis and may also help treat AIDS and cancer.

Other issues associated with genetic engineering are ethical, as people both within and outside the medical community wonder if its techniques might be used in frivolous or destructive ways. No one, however, disputes that treatments like gene therapy have already produced valuable weapons in the fight against disease and are likely to yield even more in the future. (See also BIRTH DEFECTS, **6**; GENETICS, **6**; GENETIC SCREENING, **6**; MEDICAL ETHICS, **9**.)

▶ GLOBAL WARMING

Global warming refers to a gradual change in climate that may produce higher average temperatures on earth. Although experts disagree over whether a warming trend is occurring, many predict that higher world temperatures could have a profound impact on the BIOSPHERE and on the health and survival of the life within it.

The Greenhouse Effect   Many environmentalists believe that global warming is occurring because increasing amounts of CARBON DIOXIDE (CO_2) and other gases are being released into the earth's atmosphere. Together, these gases produce what is called a greenhouse effect. Like the glass roof of a greenhouse, a layer of these gases traps the sun's heat in the earth's lower atmosphere rather than allowing it to escape into space (see illustration: The Greenhouse Effect).

Carbon dioxide is released into the air by the burning of wood and FOSSIL FUELS, such as coal, oil, gasoline, and natural gas. The level of carbon dioxide in the atmosphere has risen 30 percent since the beginning of the industrial revolution in the mid-1700s. This increase has accelerated over the past 50 years, largely because of automobile use. A second factor in this rise has been the cutting down of tropical forests in Africa

The Greenhouse Effect. *Carbon dioxide and other gases form a layer around the earth. Energy from the sun warms the earth; as this heat radiates away, it is trapped by the layer of gases in the same way that a greenhouse roof traps heat inside. A certain amount of greenhouse gases in the atmosphere is essential for survival because it makes the planet warm and livable. However, human activities such as the burning of fossil fuels have created too warm a blanket.*

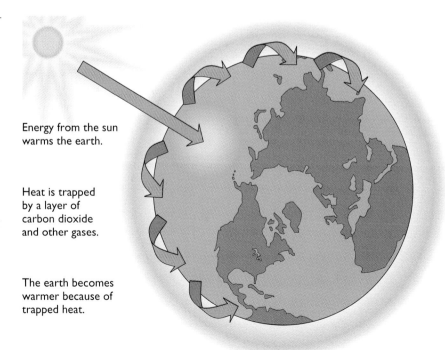

Energy from the sun warms the earth.

Heat is trapped by a layer of carbon dioxide and other gases.

The earth becomes warmer because of trapped heat.

and South America, which naturally absorb carbon dioxide, for timber and farmland. If the release of carbon dioxide and other gases continues at current levels, it has been estimated that the earth's overall average temperature will rise as much as 8°F (4.4°C) by the year 2050.

The Effects of Global Warming Scientists have predicted widespread changes that could have an impact on the health or quality of life of whole populations. Higher global temperatures would cause the polar ice caps to melt and sea levels around the world to rise, resulting in more frequent or permanent flooding of many coastal areas. Warming could also change global weather patterns, causing certain areas to receive much more rain and other areas to receive much less. Agricultural output could decline in productive regions. Among the areas predicted to receive less rain are the "breadbasket" regions of the North American and eastern Asian plains.

Another health concern is that a hotter climate could promote the spread of insects and other creatures that destroy crops or carry human diseases. Some scientists fear, for example, that northern areas might be plagued by diseases spread by insects that could not survive colder temperatures.

A Global Problem Because some degree of global warming is thought to be inevitable, many experts believe that nations should prepare for the consequences by taking such measures as developing drought-resistant plants. The degree of climate change will depend on how much carbon dioxide levels continue to rise. Governments have begun cooperative efforts to reduce the levels of greenhouse gases being released into the atmosphere by reducing the use of fossil fuels and developing other sources of energy. However, many people believe that not enough is being done to halt the destruction of tropical forests and to curtail industrial pollution and automobile use. (See also AIR POLLUTION; ENERGY CONSERVATION; OZONE; SOLAR ENERGY.)

GREENHOUSE EFFECT   see GLOBAL WARMING

GUN CONTROL   Gun control refers to state and federal laws that regulate the purchase and use of handguns, rifles, and assault weapons. Gun control laws are aimed at decreasing the use of guns to commit crimes, reducing firearm ACCIDENTS, and preventing drug addicts, criminals, and people who are mentally ill from purchasing guns.

No one knows exactly how many guns Americans own. Some estimates run as high as 200 million. It is known that they are a major cause of serious injuries and death, both accidental and purposeful. In fact, gunfire now ranks second only to auto accidents as a cause of death for Americans aged 15 to 19.

Gun Control. *Groups in favor of gun control laws are seeking greater restrictions on handguns and semiautomatic weapons.*

Gun control laws vary from state to state. For example, some states require a waiting period and background check of the buyer, some states forbid the purchase of guns through mail-order catalogs, and some states ban the purchase and ownership of guns like semiautomatic rifles. Although state laws concerning gun ownership vary, they are generally much more relaxed than in most of the world. Many countries severely limit gun ownership, viewing it as a closely guarded privilege rather than a universal right.

In the United States, many people believe that the Second Amendment of the Constitution ensures their legal right to own guns. The U.S. Supreme Court and state courts, however, have ruled that the Second Amendment primarily gives states the right to organize and maintain armed militias.

Attempts to pass tougher gun control laws have generated much debate. The *National Rifle Association (NRA),* an organization promoting the legal uses of firearms, has effectively lobbied against much proposed gun control legislation. The NRA and other groups opposed to gun control believe that state and federal laws place undue restrictions on law-abiding citizens seeking to buy or own firearms. Furthermore, these groups argue, gun control laws do not prevent criminals from possessing illegal firearms. Instead, the laws should include stiff mandatory penalties for people convicted of crimes involving the use of guns.

Nevertheless, opinion polls show that most Americans favor more restrictions on the sale and possession of handguns. Organizations like Handgun Control, Inc., oppose the NRA viewpoint. They seek a variety of nationwide regulations, including a ban on handguns and semiautomatic weapons and the institution of a waiting period and police background check to screen all gun buyers. They believe that by reducing the number of privately owned firearms—especially handguns—the rate of gun-related injuries, murders, and accidental deaths will be greatly reduced. (See also HOMICIDE.)

> ▶ **HAZARDOUS WASTE**   Hazardous waste is any type of toxic, corrosive, flammable, or irritant refuse material that can cause serious harm to human health and the environment. Hazardous waste includes such materials as household chemicals, cleaning fluids, battery acids, chemicals used in industrial processes, pesticides, and radioactive wastes (see chart: Common Hazardous Wastes and Their Effects). The unsafe disposal of hazardous wastes is a very serious public health and environmental problem.

Each year, hundreds of millions of tons of hazardous wastes are produced in the United States, but only about 10 percent of these wastes are disposed of safely. The rest are dumped in landfills or left in warehouses on the land or are dumped in lakes and rivers. Experts estimate that there are more than 30,000 dump sites around the United States that contain toxic substances. Such uncontrolled dumping can have tragic consequences on human health. Many hazardous waste materials are known to contribute to cancer and cause damage to the heart, liver, and other organs. Exposure to hazardous wastes can also cause burns, birth defects, and miscarriages.

RISK FACTORS

COMMON HAZARDOUS WASTES AND THEIR EFFECTS

Substance	Use	Effect on health
Benzene	Solvent	May cause cancer
Benzidine	Dye	Causes cancer
Carbon tetrachloride	Solvent	Highly toxic; may cause cancer
DDT	Pesticide	Highly toxic
Lead	Many uses	Highly toxic; may cause cancer
Mercury	Many uses	Highly toxic
PCBs (polychlorinated biphenyls)	Electrical circuitry, insulators, and paints	Highly toxic; may cause cancer
TCE (trichloroethylene)	Degreaser	May cause cancer
Tris	Fire retardant	May cause cancer
Vinyl chloride	Plastics	Causes cancer

Only in recent years has the public become aware of such dangers and put greater pressure on governments to deal with the problem.

Incineration and Treatment There are several ways of handling hazardous wastes to make them less dangerous. One method is incineration, or controlled burning at very high temperatures. Although incineration is effective in destroying some hazardous substances and reducing their volume, it is also very expensive. Another method for handling certain hazardous wastes is chemical or biological treatment. Chemical treatment involves adding chemical agents to hazardous materials that convert toxins to nontoxic substances or into forms that are more easily managed. Biological treatment relies on microorganisms that eat and metabolize chemicals, transforming them into harmless substances.

Burial and Storage Another method of dealing with hazardous wastes is to dispose of them in special burial sites. A relatively inexpensive "cap and contain" approach encloses toxic substances within clay or other containers that are then buried in the ground. Unfortunately, the toxic substances may eventually penetrate the barriers and seep outward, contaminating soil and water. At present, there are only a few sites in the United States that are authorized to accept toxic wastes for burial in this manner. Also, because of public opposition to the disposal of hazardous wastes, the number of such dump sites is decreasing.

A final method of dealing with hazardous wastes is to store them until better means of treatment and disposal become available. Although temporary storage is one of the least desirable methods, many hazardous wastes are now being stored because of treatment costs and opposition to disposal.

Radioactive Waste An especially dangerous type of hazardous waste is radioactive waste from NUCLEAR POWER plants and nuclear weapons factories. Even low levels of exposure to RADIATION can be extremely harmful to human health and the environment. Moreover, radioactive materials can take hundreds of thousands or even millions of years to decay naturally to the point at which they are relatively harmless. Radioactive waste therefore poses not only an immediate threat to health, but also a threat far into the future. So far, scientists have found no permanent and safe way to dispose of radioactive wastes. Burial may be dangerous because no one knows how changes in the earth's surface thousands or millions of years from now will affect burial sites. French scientists are developing a process called *vitrification* in which radioactive wastes are mixed with molten glass to produce a stable (though radioactive) solid. This solid could then be buried. At present, there are no methods available for treating radioactive wastes to make them harmless. As a result, most radioactive wastes are being stored temporarily alongside nuclear reactors or at other relatively secure locations until scientists can devise solutions to the problem.

Government and Individual Action   In the 1970s, the United States created SUPERFUND, which provided money for the cleanup of hazardous waste dump sites all around the United States. Superfund has only scratched the surface of the problem of cleanup of such sites, however. The government has also passed laws to regulate the disposal of a number of hazardous wastes. Some communities hold hazardous waste cleanup days on which individuals can bring household wastes like batteries and pesticides for careful disposal. (See also LEAD; TOXIC SUBSTANCES.)

▶ **HEATSTROKE**

Exercising Carefully.   *In hot weather, individuals should rest frequently and drink plenty of liquids to replace the fluids lost through perspiration. On very hot days, exercising less strenuously or during a cooler part of the day may be necessary.*

Heatstroke, also called sunstroke, is a medical emergency that occurs when the natural cooling mechanism of the body fails to function and BODY TEMPERATURE rises rapidly. Heatstroke usually occurs in hot, humid weather and most often affects the elderly, persons who are obese, or individuals who are exercising strenuously. (See also SPORTS AND HEAT PROBLEMS, **4.**)

Symptoms and Complications   The first symptoms of heatstroke are cessation of sweating and skin that is dry, red, and very hot. Other symptoms include a rapid heartbeat, shallow breathing, grogginess, confusion and, sometimes, coma and death. The failure to sweat makes body temperature rise quickly to 105°F (41°C) or more, which can damage vital organs of the body.

Treatment   Heatstroke requires immediate emergency assistance to cool the body, replace lost fluids, and monitor heartbeat and breathing. Until assistance arrives, the individual should be moved out of the sun and into a cool place. Spraying or sponging the person's body with cool water should be started at once to help lower body temperature. The person may also be placed in front of a fan to speed cooling. If possible, those giving first aid should monitor the individual's temperature and stop cooling measures when temperature reaches 102°F (39°C). In some cases, CPR (cardiopulmonary resuscitation) is required.

Prevention   To prevent heatstroke, take special precautions during very hot and humid weather. These include wearing light clothing, avoiding overexposure to the sun, and drinking plenty of liquids to replace fluids

HEALTHY CHOICES

lost in sweating. It may be necessary to stop exercising, adjust to a less strenuous schedule, or exercise during a cooler part of the day. (See also FIRST AID.)

▷ **HEIMLICH MANEUVER**   The Heimlich maneuver is an emergency first aid technique used to dislodge an obstruction from the throat of a person who is choking. People who are CHOKING cannot breathe, cough, or talk. They can lose consciousness and die within minutes. This simple technique has saved thousands of lives since it was developed in the 1970s by Dr. Henry Heimlich.

To perform the Heimlich maneuver, stand behind the choking person and wrap your arms around his or her torso. Clench a fist and place it, thumb-side inward, in the middle of the abdomen, below the ribs and above the navel (see illustration: The Heimlich Maneuver). Clasp the fist

The Heimlich Maneuver. *Different forms and variations.*

The Heimlich maneuver is usually performed from a standing position. From the rear, the rescuer places a fist against the victim's abdomen just above the navel and pulls sharply inward and upward four times. The maneuver is repeated as necessary.

If the person who is choking loses consciousness, the Heimlich maneuver should be performed on the floor. The rescuer straddles the victim's knees, places the hands above the victim's navel, and thrusts upward toward the head and inward, repeating as necessary.

If a baby or small child is choking, the rescuer sits down and places the baby across the lap and strikes the child firmly between the shoulder blades.

If the choking person is pregnant or obese, the rescuer's arms should be wrapped around the victim's chest, not the abdomen. The rescuer places a fist on the middle of the breastbone and pulls quickly and forcefully four times without squeezing the ribs.

with your other hand, and pull it sharply inward and upward four times. The thrust forces air out of the person's lungs and moves the blockage.

It may be necessary to repeat the technique 6 to 10 times to dislodge the object. A person who is alone and choking can also perform the technique by placing a fist covered by the other hand on the abdomen and giving a similar thrust. If this does not work, press your stomach forcefully over a chair, table, counter, or sink.

A choking person who has lost consciousness and fallen to the floor should be laid on his or her back. The Heimlich maneuver can be performed on the floor by putting the heel of one hand on the abdomen, clasping the back of that hand with the other hand, and then thrusting upward toward the head and inward (see illustration: The Heimlich Maneuver).

A variation of the Heimlich maneuver is performed on babies: Place the child face down across your lap, and sharply pat the back between the shoulder blades (see illustration: The Heimlich Maneuver). Another variation is performed on adults who are pregnant or obese: From behind the person, place the fist on the middle of the breastbone (not over the abdomen) and give four quick thrusts (see illustration: The Heimlich Maneuver).

Never use the Heimlich maneuver if choking is not actually occurring; the force of the thrust can cause injury. The Heimlich maneuver should be used only in emergencies and only for choking. Choking can look similar to other problems, such as heart attack. Ask the person if he or she can breathe. A person who is choking will be unable to talk, have difficulty breathing, and may point to or put a hand on his or her throat to give the universal choking signal. (See also CPR.)

··

► **HEMORRHAGE** see BLEEDING

··

► **HOME SAFETY** Home safety involves a number of precautions that can help prevent INJURIES and deaths caused by home ACCIDENTS. Each year in the United States, more than 3 million disabling accidents occur in the home, causing more than 21,000 deaths. The major causes of home accidents are falls, fires, and poisoning.

Household Falls Falls lead the list of home accidents. Older adults are more likely than children or younger adults to suffer serious injuries in a fall, so extra care should be taken when an older adult lives in the home. Falls can be minimized by following some common-sense guidelines:

> ► Keep stairways in good repair and free of clutter at all times. Provide adequate lighting and sturdy handrails.
> ► In the bathroom, use nonslip mats or strips in bathtubs and showers.

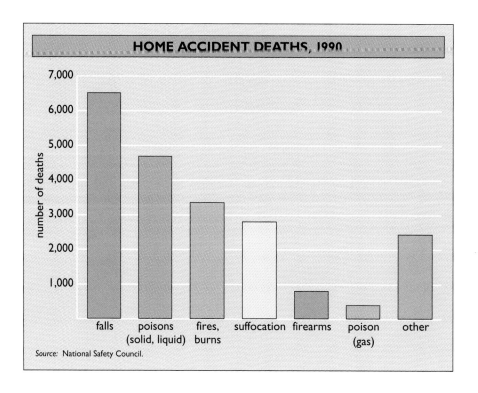

HOME ACCIDENT DEATHS, 1990

Source: National Safety Council.

► Keep a solidly built step stool in the kitchen for reaching high objects. Clean up water and food spills promptly to prevent slipping.
► Keep the yard neat by putting garden tools and toys away. Check the condition of ladders and step stools regularly, and keep them in good repair. (See also ACCESS FOR PEOPLE WITH DISABILITIES.)

Electrical Injuries The following precautions will help prevent shocks, injury, and deaths caused by electricity and electrical tools and appliances:

► Use electrical equipment correctly. For example, grasp the plug, not the cord, when unplugging an appliance, and use grounded three-pronged outlets for three-pronged plugs. Keep electrical equipment in good repair by replacing worn, frayed cords and worn plugs.
► Avoid using any electrical equipment in a damp area or near standing water. Installing special safety devices in outlets can prevent severe or fatal ELECTRIC SHOCKS. (See also ELECTRICAL SAFETY.)

Fires in the Home Fires are another major cause of accidents in the home. The following safety measures can help prevent home fires:

► Keep fire extinguishers handy in the kitchen, workroom, and near stairways and fireplaces.
► Install smoke detectors on every floor. For upper-story bedrooms, install fire ladders or other means of escape. Establish and practice an escape route for members of the household.

► When cooking, make sure that grease doesn't come in contact with flames or heat sources. Learn how to extinguish common household fires.

‣ Discard potentially flammable materials, and store flammable liquids, such as gasoline and paint, properly. (See also BURNS; FIRE SAFETY.)

Children's Accidents   When young children are in the home, special precautions are necessary.

HEALTHY CHOICES

‣ Cover unused outlets with plastic safety covers so that children can't stick their fingers or objects into the outlets.
‣ Turn the handles of pots and pans toward the back of the stove.
‣ Purchase flame-resistant pajamas and blankets. Make sure cribs meet current safety guidelines and that the crib has no sharp edges or lead-based paint.
‣ Keep cleaning supplies, plastic bags, kitchen knives, drugs, medicines, and matches out of children's reach. Teach children never to play with matches or fire. Any guns in the home should be stored, without ammunition, in a locked storage cabinet. (See also FIRST AID; POISON-CONTROL CENTERS; POISONING.)

▷ HOMICIDE

RISK FACTORS
▶ ▶ ▶ ▶ ▶ ▶

Homicide is the killing of one person by another. Homicide includes the criminal acts of murder and manslaughter as well as accidental killings and those that are legally excusable or justifiable. Homicides are a very serious public health concern in the United States because they claim so many lives each year. The widespread availability of firearms, the high incidence of SPOUSE ABUSE and CHILD ABUSE, and the increase in drug-related killings all contribute to a high homicide rate, especially in urban areas.

Homicide is the ninth leading cause of death overall in the United States. Among people aged 15 to 19, homicide committed by firearm (particularly handguns) is the second leading cause of death; for black men in that age range, it is the most frequent cause. About 25,700 criminal homicides occurred in the United States in 1990, a rate of 9.4 per 100,000 population. This rate represented a 9.3 percent increase since 1986 (see graph: Homicide Rate, 1982–1990).

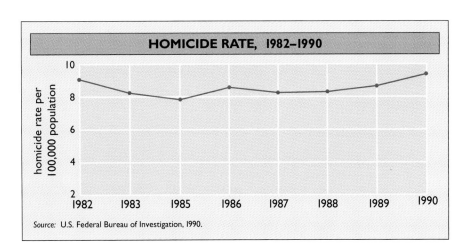

HOMICIDE RATE, 1982–1990

homicide rate per 100,000 population

Source: U.S. Federal Bureau of Investigation, 1990.

Types of Homicide   When homicide is a crime, it is called either murder or manslaughter. *Murder* generally refers to a homicide that has been committed intentionally and with "malice," or wicked purpose. *Manslaughter,* which can be intentional or unintentional, is a homicide committed without malice. It includes acts committed rashly and without forethought and accidents that result from extreme negligence. Drunk drivers who accidentally kill others are often charged with manslaughter.

Noncriminal types of homicide include justifiable and excusable homicides. A justifiable homicide is one committed within certain legal rights, such as in self-defense or to prevent a serious crime. An excusable homicide is one committed accidentally and without serious negligence. (See also GUN CONTROL; VIOLENCE.)

HYPOTHERMIA

Hypothermia is a drop in BODY TEMPERATURE to below 95°F (35°C). The normal healthy body operates with an internal temperature of approximately 98.6°F (37°C). The symptoms of mild hypothermia are shivering, which progresses to slurred speech, paleness, and listless, confused behavior. Severe hypothermia causes unconsciousness, and the heartbeat becomes faint and irregular and can eventually stop, causing death. The most common causes of hypothermia are prolonged exposure to extremely cold weather or water and contact with wet clothing in chilling weather.

RISK FACTORS
▶ ▶ ▶ ▶ ▶ ▶

Hypothermia frequently affects the homeless or those living in poorly heated quarters during periods of cold weather. Babies, whose internal regulatory systems are immature, and the elderly, who tend to be

Treatment for Hypothermia.
Mild-to-moderate cases of hypothermia should be treated by warming the person gradually.

less sensitive to changes in temperature and whose bodies are less able to adjust to cold, are at particular risk of hypothermia. Also at higher risk are people who are hungry, tired, under the influence of alcohol, or diabetic.

Treatment and Prevention   People suffering from hypothermia should be placed in a sheltered location, and any wet clothing should be removed and replaced with dry clothing. They should be wrapped in blankets, covering all the extremities including the head, and given warm, nonalcoholic liquids (see illustration: Treatment for Hypothermia). Warming should be gradual so as not to overstrain the heart, particularly in the elderly. In cases of severe hypothermia, the patient should be hospitalized as soon as possible.

HEALTHY CHOICES
●●●●●●●●●●●

The best prevention for hypothermia is to avoid prolonged exposure to extremely cold weather. When you must spend time outside in such conditions, dress appropriately and wear a hat. (See also FROSTBITE.)

▶ **INJURIES**

Injuries include damage to any part of the body. Common types of injuries and their treatment are described below.

Minor Wounds   Scrapes and scratches that cause little or no BLEEDING can be treated by washing thoroughly with soap and water to remove any dirt. Small WOUNDS can be left exposed to the air; larger wounds should be covered with a sterile dressing. Antibiotic ointments and antiseptics are usually not necessary; some (like iodine) may actually damage the skin. Bruises can be treated by applying cold compresses.

CONSULT A
PHYSICIAN

Severe Wounds   Incisions, lacerations, puncture wounds, or other wounds that are large or deep, that continue to bleed, or that show signs of infection require medical attention. Treatment may include suturing (stitching), specialized surgical techniques, and administration of antibiotics to prevent infection.

CONSULT A
PHYSICIAN

Bites and Stings   Minor animal bites should be cleaned thoroughly with soap and running water for at least 5 minutes. A bite that breaks the skin and involves a deep puncture wound or continues to bleed should be treated by a physician. To determine whether the injured person has been exposed to rabies, the animal must be confined and observed for 7 to 10 days. (See also RABIES, **2**.)

CONSULT A
PHYSICIAN

Minor insect bites can be treated by carefully removing the stinger (if necessary), washing the area with soap and water, and applying a paste of baking soda, a wet cloth, or a cold compress to reduce pain. Over-the-counter hydrocortisone cream can help reduce itching and inflammation. Allergic reactions to any bite and serious bites from insects, scorpions, and poisonous spiders or snakes require immediate medical attention. (See also BITES AND STINGS.)

Sprains and Strains   These injuries occur when joints or muscles are twisted or stretched beyond their normal range of motion. Symptoms may include pain and tenderness; rapid swelling, sometimes accompanied by skin discoloration; and impaired function. Minor injuries can be

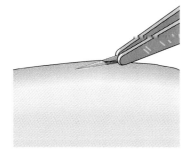

Removing a Splinter.

treated with RICE (rest, ice, compression, and elevation). Serious SPRAINS AND STRAINS should be treated by a physician.

Splinters and Other Foreign Objects A splinter can be removed from the skin with tweezers that have been dipped in rubbing alcohol or disinfectant. In some cases, foreign objects in the eyes, ears, or nose can be removed without professional assistance. If something is in the eyes it may be possible to flush it out with a small amount of clean water. Never rub the eyes. Objects in the ear can often be removed with tweezers or gently dislodged by tilting the head to the affected side and shaking it gently. If these methods fail, seek medical assistance immediately.

Burns Skin injuries caused by fire, the sun, chemicals, hot objects or fluids, and ELECTRIC SHOCK result in injuries that range from minor to serious, depending on the extent of damage to the skin. Minor BURNS can be treated with cool, running water. Severe burns require medical assistance. (See also DISLOCATIONS; FIRST AID; FRACTURES; FROSTBITE.)

LEAD

Lead-Based Paint. *Lead-based paint is a significant environmental danger in many American homes. Exposure to lead-laced dust can cause impairment of intelligence, memory, and other mental functions in children.*

Lead is a poisonous metal present in such things as old paint, leaded gasoline, and some water supply pipes. When ingested or inhaled, it can cause nervous system and kidney damage and inhibit the body's ability to form red blood cells. Lead accumulates in the body tissues, so exposure to even relatively small amounts over a period of time can cause serious problems. In the household, sources of lead contamination in food and water include lead plumbing, lead-glazed pottery, leaded crystal, and many imported wines, which may use a lead seal.

Lead is particularly harmful to fetuses and children. Lead poisoning in children is commonly caused by lead-based paint in older homes (see illustration: Lead-Based Paint). Children have been known to eat peeling paint chips. An equally great danger to children in homes with old paint, however, is inhaling lead particles in household dust.

The U.S. government banned lead paint in 1977 and is still phasing out the use of lead in gasoline. This has greatly reduced the amount of lead in the environment. Precautions against overexposure to lead include having household drinking water tested, avoiding the use of imported or old lead-glazed pottery (brightly colored and glossy) for serving food, and having the family stay elsewhere when an old home is being renovated to avoid breathing lead paint dust. (See also AIR POLLUTION; HAZARDOUS WASTE; PARTICULATES; TOXIC SUBSTANCES.)

MEDICAL SELF-CARE

Medical self-care involves the measures that people practice at home to maintain their own health and the health of their families. Many minor illnesses can be cared for at home without visiting a doctor or with a doctor's supervision and advice. Some chronic conditions, such as diabetes, ulcers, arthritis, and kidney diseases, also require ongoing care that can often be carried out at home.

Self-Care Reference Books and Equipment Every home should include authoritative reference books for information on the diagnosis and treatment of minor illnesses such as colds, flu, fever, and childhood illnesses. Family medical guides that describe illnesses and common symptoms are useful, and books on prescription and nonprescription drugs can identify medications and provide information about their side effects. If an infant is part of the household, a good baby-care book is also advisable.

An oral or rectal thermometer is an important diagnostic tool. It is used to measure BODY TEMPERATURE to determine if a fever is present. It is also important to know how to take a *pulse,* or heart rate. By knowing baseline measurements of vital signs like temperature and heart rate, it is easier to detect the onset of illness. Normal temperature is about 98.6°F; a normal pulse is about 60 to 80 beats per minute, although it is usually faster for children and slower for athletes. Medical self-care for someone recuperating from a serious illness or someone with a chronic illness may require more specialized knowledge and equipment. The patient may need a hospital bed, walker, wheelchair, commode (portable toilet), bedpan, or adjustable bed table. Examples of health-care routines that can be performed at home include administering medication and maintaining medication schedules, assisting with physical therapy, preparing special foods, and taking vital signs.

When to Call the Doctor Part of a good medical self-care regimen is knowing when to call the doctor. The doctor's number as well as the numbers for police, fire, and POISON-CONTROL CENTER should be kept beside the telephone. The doctor should be called when the patient has a high fever, a fever that doesn't break within a day or so, or persistent symptoms that do not respond to medication. If a family member has trouble breathing, loses consciousness, or suffers a severe injury, emergency medical personnel should be summoned immediately. (See also FIRST AID; HOME HEALTH SERVICES, **9.**)

CONSULT A PHYSICIAN

▷ **MERCURY**   **see** TOXIC SUBSTANCES

▷ **MOTION SICKNESS**   Motion sickness is a condition caused by repeated movement, such as may occur during road, sea, or air travel. Mild symptoms include headache and uneasiness; in more severe cases, sweating, nausea, and vomiting may occur. Researchers believe motion sickness results from contradictory sensory messages: The organ of balance in the inner ear detects movements and changes in body position, but the eyes experience a still environment. Children are more frequently affected by motion sickness than are adults. The reaction to movement becomes less common with age as the organ of balance becomes less sensitive to movement.

RELIEVING MOTION SICKNESS

To help relieve motion sickness

▶ Brace your head during a journey, preferably while lying down.

▶ Do not read.

▶ Stay in the center of the car, boat, or plane.

▶ Consume small amounts of food and drink at regular intervals.

▶ Avoid alcohol.

▶ Focus on the horizon or fixed points in the distance.

To help prevent motion sickness, over-the-counter antihistamines (Dramamine and Benadryl) can be taken prior to travel. Stronger medications, including a type administered through a skin patch, are available by prescription. These drugs cause drowsiness, however, and should not be used by anyone who plans to drive. Once motion sickness has started, several strategies may help to relieve its symptoms (see chart: Relieving Motion Sickness).

▶ **MOTORCYCLE SAFETY**   Motorcycle safety involves a number of precautions that can help prevent injury and death. These safety guidelines address two main problems: Motorcycles are less visible than other vehicles on the road, and the riders of motorcycles and mopeds have no protection in the event of a collision. In fact, the driver of a motorcycle is five times more likely to be killed in an accident than is the driver of an automobile.

Wear Protective Gear   Motorcyclists should always wear an approved helmet as well as a face shield or goggles. Clothing is also important: Leather jackets provide protection against wind and cold; long pants and boots shield legs from muffler burns and weather; and gloves protect the hands.

Drive Safely and Defensively   Motorcyclists must follow rules of the road that apply to all motor vehicles and use extra caution in wet conditions. They should practice riding techniques, such as braking on wet roads and leaning into the bends, on quiet roads before using them on busy highways. Motorcyclists should never assume that other drivers can see the bike. Instead they should use their headlights and horn to make others aware of them.

Protective Motorcycle Gear.
Motorcyclists can reduce their chances of serious injury by wearing appropriate clothing and safety equipment. This includes a helmet, leather jacket, long pants, and leather boots.

Choose a Motorcycle Carefully   A person buying a motorcycle should select one for its safety rather than its speed. It should be a bike that the rider can handle with confidence and ease. Anyone buying a second-hand motorcycle should get an expert's opinion on the condition of the machine, especially the tires, brakes, wheel and steering bearings, chain, exhaust system, lights, and engine. (See also ACCIDENTS; AUTOMOBILE SAFETY.)

▷ **MOUTH-TO-MOUTH RESUSCITATION**   see CPR

▷ **NOISE POLLUTION**   Noise pollution is any loud or annoying sound that is present in a person's environment. The sound of traffic, loud radios, airplane engines, lawn mowers, passing trains, fire sirens, even barking dogs are all potential sources of noise pollution. Prolonged exposure to loud noises affects a person's health and may cause hearing loss.

    Loudness is measured in units called *decibels*. A soft whisper measures about 30 decibels, traffic between 50 and 70 decibels, and a jet taking off about 130 decibels (see chart: Noise Levels in the Environment). Generally, the louder and higher the pitch of a sound, the more annoying and unpleasant it is likely to be.

Physical and Psychological Effects   Noise is a major physical and psychological stressor. When people are exposed to loud noise, they experience increases in blood pressure, heart and respiration rates, cholesterol and hormone levels, and muscle tension. Exposure to noises of 85 decibels or more for a prolonged period can cause *sensory deafness*. In this condition, tiny hairs and muscles in the ear become fatigued and eventually stop functioning altogether.

    Noise affects people's emotions as well, producing annoyance and irritability. Workplace noise decreases productivity and the ability to concentrate. Some studies even suggest a link between excessive noise and high workplace ACCIDENT rates. Studies have shown that even when people have become accustomed to loud noise and no longer consciously hear it, these physical and emotional changes still occur.

HEALTHY CHOICES   **Protecting Against Noise Pollution**   People can reduce the effects of noise pollution by using earplugs or ear protectors when operating loud machinery and by soundproofing rooms with sound-absorbing building materials and furnishings like upholstery and drapes. Many communities have adopted noise-reduction ordinances to control the noise level from

NOISE LEVELS IN THE ENVIRONMENT		
Sound	**Noise level in decibels**	**Individual perception**
Soft whisper	30	Very quiet
Light traffic	50	Quiet/moderate
Normal conversation	60	
Highway traffic	65–70	Loud/intrusive
Shouting, arguing	80	Very loud/annoying
Lawn mower	90	
Garbage truck	100	
Amplified rock music	110–120	Extremely loud
Jet takeoff (200 feet)	120–140	Painful

such nuisances as machinery and blaring radios. Some airports have changed takeoff and approach patterns to reduce noise to surrounding areas. (See also EAR, **1**; HEARING LOSS, **3**.)

▶ NONSMOKERS' RIGHTS

Nonsmokers' rights refers to the conviction that nonsmokers have the right not to be exposed to cigarette smoke from the smokers around them. This belief is backed by national, state, and local laws and policies that ban or greatly restrict smoking in public places and on the job.

The Dangers of Smoking   In the years before the health risks of smoking were known, a concept of nonsmokers' rights did not exist. In 1964, the United States Surgeon General issued a report linking smoking with lung cancer and other serious diseases. As education about the dangers of smoking became more available, smoking became less acceptable. Then a 1986 surgeon general's report showed that *sidestream smoke* (smoke from the burning end of a cigarette that along with exhaled smoke is known as *secondhand smoke*) was also very dangerous. In fact, it contained higher concentrations of various poisons and carcinogens (cancer-causing agents) than did the smoke inhaled by smokers. Nonsmokers became increasingly concerned about the health risks of *passive smoking,* or breathing secondhand smoke.

RISK FACTORS
▶ ▶ ▶ ▶ ▶ ▶

Many studies in recent years have found that passive smoking by spouses of smokers puts them at a greater risk than spouses of nonsmokers for developing heart disease and lung cancer. Passive smoking by the children of smokers makes these children more likely than other children to suffer from respiratory diseases.

Laws About Smoking   In 1974, the National Interagency Council on Smoking and Health adopted a "Nonsmokers' Bill of Rights," which expressed the view that nonsmokers had the right to breathe clean air and

Smoking Restrictions. *Smoking is already restricted in many public places as well as in many workplaces.*

to lobby for nonsmoking laws. That same year, Arizona passed the first state no-smoking law regulating smoking in public places. By 1988, more than 40 states and 370 cities and counties had also passed smoking restriction laws. Smoking has been banned on all domestic airline flights and in certain areas of federal buildings.

State and local laws vary, but most restrict or ban smoking in all enclosed public places including elevators, hospitals, and movie theaters. In some places, smoking is prohibited in restaurants; in others, there must be separate areas for smokers and nonsmokers. Public opinion polls show that more than three-fourths of Americans, including smokers, support restrictions on smoking in public places.

► NUCLEAR POWER

Nuclear power is electrical energy produced by the fission (or splitting) of uranium atoms within a *nuclear reactor.* Over the past 30 years, nuclear power plants have become an increasingly important source of energy for nations around the world. Nuclear power poses a potential threat, however, to human health because of the possible release of RADIATION into the environment.

In the United States, nuclear power generates roughly one-sixth of the nation's power. In Europe, nuclear power is generally more common. France, for example, gets nearly two-thirds of its electricity from nuclear sources.

How Nuclear Power Works Nuclear reactors generate tremendous heat by breaking up the nuclei of radioactive uranium atoms. This heat produces steam, which is then pumped into turbines connected to electric generators.

Supporters of nuclear power believe that it offers significant advantages over FOSSIL FUELS such as coal, natural gas, and oil. The energy

Chernobyl. *On April 26, 1986, a malfunction in the cooling system of the Chernobyl nuclear power plant in the former Soviet Union led to a meltdown and the worst explosion in nuclear power's short history. The reactor is now encased in concrete to prevent further leakage of radiation.*

released through nuclear fission is more than a million times greater than that obtained from the burning of an equivalent mass of fossil fuels. With the ever-increasing demand for electricity, a reliable, abundant source of power is of great importance. Nuclear power plants are also a relatively clean source of electricity—that is, they produce none of the AIR POLLUTION that fossil fuels do. For this reason, nuclear power gained widespread acceptance as an alternative to traditional forms of energy throughout the 1960s and 1970s.

Risks of Nuclear Power   Many people are concerned about the dangers related to the generation of nuclear power, however. Two major *nuclear accidents* have dramatized the potential health hazard it poses. The first occurred at the Three Mile Island nuclear power plant near Harrisburg, Pennsylvania, in March 1979. The plant's cooling system malfunctioned, allowing large quantities of radioactive gas and steam to escape into the atmosphere. There were no deaths from the accident, but people at the plant and in surrounding areas were exposed to high levels of radiation.

In 1986, a much more serious accident occurred at the Chernobyl nuclear power plant in the former Soviet Union. The uranium rods in the core of the reactor overheated and melted (a situation called a *meltdown*), triggering an explosion that blew the roof off the building housing the reactor. This showered the surrounding area with radioactive particles; winds carried dangerous levels of radiation outside the Soviet Union. A number of plant workers died immediately. Other workers and people in the surrounding area developed *radiation sickness*, characterized by symptoms such as hair loss, vomiting, diarrhea, and the development of leukemia. The health consequences of Chernobyl, including possible birth defects, may continue to be felt for years.

Even when nuclear power plants are operating safely, disposing of the radioactive wastes produced by the process presents a serious problem. Most of these wastes remain radioactive for hundreds and even thousands of years. They are stored in special containment vessels and may be buried deep underground. Leakage from these containment vessels is a potential danger.

During the past several years, scientists have come up with a design for a safer, gas-cooled nuclear reactor, which they claim would greatly reduce the risk of an accident. In France, scientists are developing a process called *vitrification* to help solve the problem of radioactive waste disposal. This involves mixing radioactive wastes with molten glass to produce a stable (though radioactive) solid. This material could then be buried safely deep in the ground. (See also HAZARDOUS WASTE; SOLAR ENERGY.)

> Many people are concerned about the dangers related to the generation of nuclear power. Two major nuclear accidents have dramatized the potential health hazard it poses.

▶ OCCUPATIONAL SAFETY AND HEALTH ADMINISTRATION

The Occupational Safety and Health Administration, usually called OSHA, is a federal agency that promotes safe and healthful working conditions. The main responsibilities of the agency, which is part of the U.S. Department of Labor, are developing and enforcing job safety and health regulations and educating employers and employees about hazards in the workplace.

OSHA Inspections. *OSHA inspectors check workplaces to be sure government regulations are being followed. Employers who fail to conform to regulations may be fined.*

OSHA was established in 1970 by the Williams-Steiger Occupational Health and Safety Act. Since then, it has developed regulations about environmental health and safety hazards in places of employment. These hazards include any chemical, biological, or physical stresses that can cause illness or injury to employees. The agency establishes guidelines for maximum levels of exposure to TOXIC SUBSTANCES, including ASBESTOS and LEAD. Examples of other areas governed by OSHA regulations include fire prevention, protective clothing for workers, and such matters as placement of safety railings and emergency exits. OSHA inspectors check places of employment to make sure regulations are being followed. Employers that fail to make changes to meet OSHA standards are fined.

With the encouragement of OSHA, many states have developed their own health and safety programs. State programs that are approved by OSHA receive partial funding from the federal government. (See also ACCIDENTS; ENVIRONMENTAL ORGANIZATIONS; FIRE SAFETY; SAFETY EQUIPMENT; SAFETY ON THE JOB.)

▶ **OIL SPILLS**

An oil spill is the discharge of oil, most commonly into oceans or other waterways. A spill may result from such things as an oil tanker accident, a leaking oil well or pipeline, or the intentional discharge of oil from a ship. Because oil is toxic, oil spills are a major WATER POLLUTION threat in many regions of the world. They pose a serious threat to ocean ecosystems as well as to human health.

Millions of gallons of oil are spilled into the environment each year. One of the worst oil spills in recent years involved the oil tanker *Exxon Valdez,* which spilled more than 10 million gallons of oil into Alaska's

Cleaning Oil Spills. *Oil spills are difficult to clean up entirely, and their toxic effects can linger for years.*

Prince William Sound in 1989. Such spills can have a devastating effect on marine life. Fish, sea birds, and aquatic mammals may die within a short time after oil fouls their environment. Oil spills are nearly impossible to clean up entirely, and their toxic effects can linger for years.

Some experts believe that increased quantities of oil in the oceans will eventually lead to the biological breakdown of many plant and animal species. In addition, everything spilled into the oceans eventually ends up in the food chain, where it may contaminate human food supplies and adversely affect human health.

It is both difficult and costly to clean up an oil spill. If caught in time, some oil can be collected off the surface or broken up with detergents. Some disperses as a result of natural processes. Certain bacteria, for example, consume oil and eventually return polluted water to a more normal state.

Many experts believe the best solution is to take steps to lessen the chances of accidental oil spills. In the United States, legislation has been passed to try to prevent major oil spills or to make responsible companies pay for cleaning up the environment. (See also FOSSIL FUELS; TOXIC SUBSTANCES.)

▷ OZONE

Ozone is a form of oxygen that consists of three atoms of oxygen instead of the normal two. Ozone occurs naturally in the upper atmosphere, where it collects in a protective layer that shields the earth's life-forms from damaging ultraviolet (UV) RADIATION. Excessive amounts of ozone at ground level, however, can act as a harmful pollutant. Unfortunately, the effects of AIR POLLUTION are depleting ozone in the upper atmosphere, where it is beneficial, and producing too much of it in the lower atmosphere, where it can be harmful.

Ground-Level Ozone The ozone found at ground level is a by-product of motor vehicle and industrial air pollution. It is one of the components of the unhealthy SMOG that sometimes accumulates as a result of a TEMPERATURE INVERSION. The ozone in smog can be very irritating to the eyes and can damage the respiratory system. Ozone can also cause headaches, fatigue, and coughing. Efforts to decrease the amounts of gaseous air pollutants, if successful, can potentially reduce levels of ground-level ozone.

The Ozone Layer A thin layer of ozone occurs naturally in the earth's upper atmosphere. This ozone layer is crucial to the survival of plant and animal life on earth. It absorbs harmful ultraviolet radiation (the part of the sun's rays that causes sunburn and more serious disorders), keeping most of it from reaching the earth's surface.

Scientists have become increasingly concerned because the earth's ozone layer appears to be growing thinner. A primary cause of ozone depletion is the use of human-made chemical compounds called *chlorofluorocarbons*, or CFCs. CFCs are used as coolants in air conditioners and refrigerators, as solvents in the manufacturing of electronic equipment, as foaming agents in insulation and food packaging, and, until recently, as propellants in aerosol spray cans.

Ozone depletion is not constant around the world. So far, it is greatest in the polar regions, where scientists have discovered ozone holes in the layer during certain times of the year. These holes have grown larger each year and have remained longer. The ozone layer is thinning, however, throughout the middle latitudes, not merely over the poles. As a consequence, increasing levels of UV radiation have been measured in various locations worldwide.

RISK FACTORS
▶ ▶ ▶ ▶ ▶ ▶

Higher levels of UV radiation could prove harmful, even lethal, to plants and animals. Among the risks to humans are increased rates of skin cancer and cataracts, a leading cause of blindness. Studies show that increased exposure to UV radiation can also damage the body's immune system, reducing its ability to fight disease. Exposure may also have damaging genetic effects.

In the environment, increased levels of ultraviolet radiation can reduce crop yields and damage marine life. At its worst, significant depletion of the ozone layer could conceivably destroy life on Earth. (See also SKIN CANCER, **3**.)

Chlorofluorocarbons. *The CFCs routinely used in foaming agents for insulation and packaging materials will damage the Earth's ozone layer for decades.*

Preserving the Ozone Layer   Efforts are being made to control the manufacture of chemicals responsible for depletion of the ozone layer. In the past two decades, the United States and a number of other countries have agreed to sharply reduce the use of CFCs by the end of this century. Consumers can help by avoiding the use of plastic foam packaging and insulation materials, choosing energy-efficient refrigerators, and having air conditioners serviced frequently.

Even with such efforts, however, many experts believe that too little is being done too late. Current levels of CFCs could continue to destroy ozone for up to a century. The Environmental Protection Agency has estimated that more than 80 million additional cases of skin cancer will result during the next 80 years because of the damage already done to the ozone layer. Despite great speculation and active scientific research, the full effects of ozone-layer depletion on humans and the environment are not yet clear. (See also BIOSPHERE; GLOBAL WARMING.)

▶ **PARTICULATES**   Particulates are tiny solid particles suspended in the air. Some particulates are the results of natural processes, such as volcanic eruptions, but most are by-products of manufacturing and mining. Particulates include soot, ashes, coal dust, textile fibers, and fragments of metals such as LEAD. Inhaling particulates can cause or contribute to some kinds of respiratory disease and has been linked to several types of cancer.

Effects of Particulates   Cilia, tiny hairs in the human lung, are able to filter out most particulates so they can be expelled during coughing. Some particulates and gases, however, can temporarily paralyze the cilia, enabling particles to become permanently embedded in the lungs. These particles irritate the lungs, diminishing their capacity and making them

Coal Dust. *Many coal miners have developed a serious disease known as black lung, caused by years of inhaling coal dust.*

more vulnerable to mucus buildup and infection. Some particles, including ASBESTOS and tobacco residue, can cause lung cancer and emphysema.

Sources of Particulate Pollution Particulates cause AIR POLLUTION as well as indoor pollution. Industrial processes are the source of the greatest amount of particulate pollution in the air. Particulate pollution also comes from motor vehicle emissions, from deteriorating insulating or fireproofing materials, and from mold spores and dust mites. In addition, particulates in the form of pollen are produced by flowering plants. People engaged in mining and certain manufacturing are especially vulnerable to serious respiratory conditions resulting from breathing particulates. Textile fibers, coal dust, and asbestos fibers can all cause chronic, often fatal, lung diseases in unprotected workers. Pollen and mold spores cause allergic reactions in many people.

Smokestack scrubbing devices and emission control devices can cut down on the release of particulates by industry. People who work in mining, industrial, and some textile occupations need to take precautions to protect themselves against the particulates produced by their industries by wearing face masks or other safety equipment. In the United States, the Clean Air Acts have reduced industrial particulates to some extent, but they are still a major source of air pollution. (See also SAFETY ON THE JOB; ALLERGIES, 3; CANCER, 3; LUNG DISEASE, 3; SMOKING, 7.)

▶ **POISON-CONTROL CENTERS** Poison-Control Centers provide expert information and advice on the emergency treatment of POISONING. The centers are often associated with hospitals or emergency rooms and typically consist of toll-free 24-hour telephone lines as well as special libraries used by the staff. In most cases, the information provided by the staff at Poison-Control Centers makes it possible for callers to handle poisoning emergencies at home or at least provide emergency FIRST AID.

If it is suspected that a person has ingested, inhaled, or come into contact with a poisonous substance, the local Poison-Control Center should be called immediately. The number can usually be found on the inside cover of the telephone book or in the white pages, or it can be obtained from the operator. A caller will be asked questions, including name, location, and telephone number, as well as the type and amount of the substance ingested. It is important to have the substance in hand while calling so that its ingredients can be identified.

The caller will also be asked to describe the condition of the person poisoned. Is the victim conscious or unconscious, what is the overall condition, what are the symptoms, and what has already been done in an effort to help? Based on the detailed information provided, the staff member will offer specific, step-by-step instructions for first aid treatment. In serious cases, it may be necessary to take the person to a hospital emergency room for follow-up care. It is important to take the poisonous substance and any vomitus to the hospital as well. It may be necessary to analyze these at the hospital to exactly determine the type of poison.

Poison-Control Center. *The staff of poison-control centers are experts at handling poisoning emergencies.*

HEALTHY CHOICES
•••••••••••••

To save time in the event of emergency, the phone number of the Poison-Control Center should be posted near the telephone. Family members, babysitters, and others should be informed about how and when to call for assistance. (See also BITES AND STINGS; EMERGENCY CARE SERVICES; HOME SAFETY; POISONOUS PLANTS; TOXIC SUBSTANCES.)

▷ **POISONING**

A poison is any substance that, when ingested, inhaled, injected, or absorbed through the skin, interferes with the normal functioning of the body. Among the most familiar poisons are pesticides, household cleaners, petroleum products, and industrial chemicals. But almost all nonfood substances can be poisonous, if taken in large enough doses. Accidental poisoning, which occurs most often in young children, is one of the most common types of household ACCIDENTS. If immediate professional care is not provided, poisoning can result in death or permanent injury.

Symptoms of poisoning vary depending on the substance involved and the route of absorption. Corrosives, such as battery acid, caustic soda, strong antiseptics, and tincture of iodine, may produce burns and intense pain in the mouth, throat, and stomach as well as vomiting, shock, and breathing difficulties. Ingestion or inhalation of petroleum products, such as kerosene, gasoline, cleaning fluids, solvents, paint thinners, and polishes, can cause vomiting, diarrhea, headache, blurred vision, delirium, convulsions, coma, and death.

Chemicals are not the only poisonous substances, however. Food and water contaminated with bacteria and other microorganisms can cause abdominal pain, vomiting, and diarrhea. Numerous plants are toxic if eaten. POISONOUS PLANTS include mushrooms, English ivy, rhododendron, and lily-of-the-valley. Some, such as poison ivy and poison oak, produce rashes and blisters when they touch the skin, a reaction called *contact poisoning*.

RISK FACTORS
▶ ▶ ▶ ▶ ▶ ▶

Any type of drug or other medication can be toxic when taken in high doses or in combination with certain other drugs or alcohol. Aspirin

COMMON HOUSEHOLD POISONS

Acetaminophen	Houseplants	Paint thinner
Acids	Ibuprofen	Perfume
Aspirin	Insecticides	Permanent-wave solution
Bleach	Iodine	Photography chemicals
Carpet cleaner	Kerosene	Rat poison
Deodorants	Laxatives	Room deodorizer
Diet pills	Lighter fluid	Rubbing alcohol
Drain cleaner	Liquor	Sedatives
Drugs	Metal polish	Shampoo
Fabric softener	Model cement	Soaps and detergents
Fertilizers	Mothballs	Stain removers
Floor wax	Nail polish	Toilet cleaner
Furniture polish	Nail polish remover	Turpentine
Gasoline	Nose drops	Vitamins
Glue	Oven cleaner	Weed killers
Hairspray	Painkillers	Window cleaning fluid
Hair straighteners	Paint	

is one of the leading causes of accidental poisonings among children. Sleeping medications, antihistamines, and vitamin supplements are also frequently misused. The use of *childproof caps,* however, has reduced the number of accidental poisonings among children.

RISK FACTORS
▶ ▶ ▶ ▶ ▶ ▶

How Poisonings Occur Accidental poisonings can occur in a variety of ways. Most of the 7 million poisonings reported each year involve children younger than 5 years of age. Young children may mistake bottles containing household cleaners for beverages or vitamins and other medications for candy. Children are also liable to be poisoned by tasting houseplants, mushrooms, or inedible berries. Poisonings are also common among elderly people. Failing eyesight can result in misreading of labels and overdose. In addition, elderly people frequently must take several different medications, which can result in confusion and dosage mistake. Suicidal overdoses of barbiturates and other drugs are another cause of poisoning. People are also poisoned through exposure to water, soil, and air contaminated by chemicals in the workplace, especially in industrial jobs.

First Aid for Poisoning The first step in handling any poisoning emergency is usually to identify the substance involved. If the person is unable to talk, it is necessary to search for clues such as open containers, burns, and stains. Odors on the person's breath may also help to identify the substance. Next, the local POISON-CONTROL CENTER, hospital emergency room, or rescue squad should be contacted for instructions.

FIRST AID measures vary according to the poison involved and the method of absorption. A person who has swallowed a corrosive agent or a petroleum product should not be made to vomit. Instead the person should drink water or milk and wait for emergency help to arrive. If the substance ingested was not corrosive, vomiting can be induced by giving *syrup of ipecac* and water. The person should be positioned face down, with the head lower than the rest of the body.

A person who has inhaled a poisonous substance should be carried into the open air; any tight-fitting clothing should be loosened; and he or she should be wrapped in a blanket to prevent shock. If breathing and heartbeat stop, CPR should be used. If a poison has entered the eye, it should be flushed with lukewarm running water until medical help arrives. To remove poisonous substances from the skin, wash the affected area with water. Do not apply ointments or creams.

HEALTHY CHOICES

Poisoning Prevention To prevent accidental poisonings in the home, *childproofing* is essential. Hazardous chemicals as well as over-the-counter and prescription medications should be stored in locked cabinets. All substances should be left in their original containers; never transfer them to milk or soft-drink bottles, where they may be consumed by mistake.

When handling pesticides and herbicides, it is important to wear protective clothing. When taking any medication, read the label directions carefully, and do not exceed the recommended dosage. (See also AIR POLLUTION; BITES AND STINGS; CARBON MONOXIDE POISONING; HOME SAFETY; LEAD; OCCUPATIONAL SAFETY AND HEALTH ADMINISTRATION; SAFETY ON THE JOB; TOXIC SUBSTANCES; DRUG OVERDOSE, 7.)

▶ POISONOUS PLANTS

RISK FACTORS

Poisonous plants are those garden, house, and wild plants that can cause allergic skin reactions or disrupt the normal functioning of the body. Poison ivy, poison oak, and poison sumac, for example, produce an itchy, blistery rash when touched. Hundreds of other plants, including foxglove, yew, lily-of-the-valley, larkspur, mountain laurel, and a wide variety of mushrooms, can cause POISONING if eaten. In fact, plants are the second most common cause of serious poisoning in children younger than 5 years of age.

Internal Poisoning Many plants have both edible parts and poisonous parts. For example, tomato leaves, apple seeds, and the sprouts, roots, and vines of potatoes are poisonous parts of common food plants. The poisonous berries of plants like holly and bittersweet are especially enticing—and therefore dangerous—to children. Some houseplants, such as philodendron and dieffenbachia, as well as many plants that grow in gardens and in the wild are also poisonous if ingested (see chart: Poisonous Plants Found in the House or Garden).

Symptoms of internal poisoning vary from plant to plant. They may include abdominal pain, vomiting, diarrhea, breathing difficulties, delirium, and coma and can prove fatal. If a poisonous plant has been ingested, the local POISON-CONTROL CENTER should be telephoned immediately for instructions. In most cases, the person should be made to vomit. Vomiting can usually be induced by giving 1 or 2 tablespoons of *syrup of ipecac* and a glass of water. If the plant is unfamiliar, it should

POISONOUS PLANTS FOUND IN THE HOUSE OR GARDEN		
Autumn crocus	Dieffenbachia	Philodendron
Azalea	English ivy	Poinsettia
Bittersweet	Foxglove	Rhododendron
Buttercup	Holly	Skunk cabbage
Daffodil	Iris	Wisteria
Delphinium	Lily-of-the-valley	Yew

CONSULT A PHYSICIAN

be saved so that it can be identified, and both the plant and the person poisoned should be taken to an emergency care facility.

Contact Poisoning   Poison ivy, poison oak, and poison sumac are the most common sources of contact poisoning. The primary symptom is a red, itchy rash several hours or days after exposure. In some people, the rash is accompanied by generalized swelling, headache, and fever.

Aside from the characteristic three-leaf pattern, poison ivy and oak vary greatly in appearance and may be hard to recognize. People usually brush against poison ivy or poison oak while walking in the woods or working in the garden. The chemical in the oil secreted by these plants that produces the rash is called *urushiol*. This irritant may also be picked up by the fur of dogs and cats and then transferred to people. Although many people are not affected after their first or second exposure to these poisonous plants, repeated contact usually results in a rash.

If exposure occurs, remove all contaminated clothing immediately, wash the affected area thoroughly with cold water, and then sponge with alcohol. If a rash appears, calamine lotion or hydrocortisone cream can be applied to the area. If a fever or other symptoms develop, medical assistance should be sought. All contaminated clothing or other objects should be washed immediately to prevent reinfection.

HEALTHY CHOICES

People walking through woods or other areas where these plants grow should wear protective clothing and wash when they get home. Poison ivy growing in the garden can be killed with a herbicide. The dead plants should then be buried—never burned or left where people may still come in contact with them. (See also TOXIC SUBSTANCES.)

▶ **POISONPROOFING**   see HOME SAFETY

▶ **POPULATION GROWTH**   Population growth refers to increases in the total number of people occupying a particular area. Growth rates are uneven throughout the world: Most industrialized countries have stable populations or low rates of growth, while many developing countries have high rates of growth. Most experts agree that world population growth needs

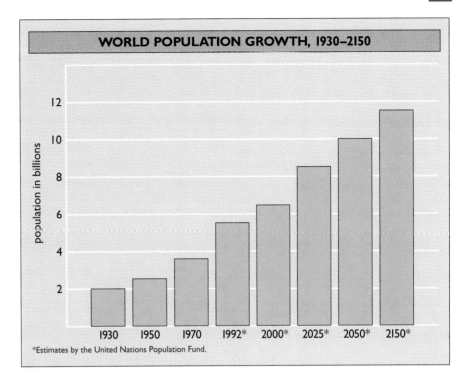

WORLD POPULATION GROWTH, 1930–2150

population in billions

*Estimates by the United Nations Population Fund.

to be controlled in order to prevent human, economic, and environmental catastrophes.

The Growth of Population For much of human history, world population grew rather slowly. In recent centuries, however, developments in agriculture, medicine, and technology have allowed populations to expand dramatically. Total world population reached 1 billion in 1850. Just 80 years later, in 1930, the world population had doubled, and by 1992 it was nearly 5.5 billion. By the year 2000, the world population is projected to reach 6 billion, and if current growth rates continue, it will probably reach 10 billion by the year 2050 (see graph: World Population Growth, 1930–2150). Most of this growth will occur in the developing nations of the world, especially those on the continent of Africa.

Dangers of Uncontrolled Growth Many experts believe that uncontrolled population growth poses a serious threat to the world's environment. In many places, rapidly expanding populations are straining the ability of the environment to provide enough food, water, housing, and fuel. In addition, forests are being destroyed at an alarming rate, contributing to the problem of GLOBAL WARMING. Overused croplands are losing their productivity, and some are becoming barren deserts. The growth of cities is contributing to AIR POLLUTION and WATER POLLUTION.

Solutions to Growth Problems Most proposed solutions to the world population problem involve controlling population growth through family planning. Many experts recommend making information on contraception more readily available, especially in developing nations. Experts also recommend the development of better birth-control methods. In addition, the social and economic problems of poorer nations need to be addressed. Greater economic development and improved living standards usually result in reduced birth rates. (See also CONTRACEPTION, **6**.)

Some experts argue that until population is brought under control, industrialized nations must help poorer nations learn to manage their resources and protect the environment. Otherwise, these nations will face poverty and hunger, and local and global environments may be severely damaged for years to come.

▶ PRESSURE-POINT TECHNIQUE   see BLEEDING

▶ PULSE

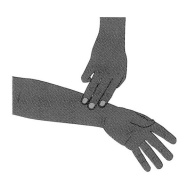

Taking a Pulse. *The wrist is the most common place to take a pulse. It can be taken by placing the middle fingers of the hand gently on the wrist just below the base of the thumb. Count the number of beats in 15 seconds and multiply by 4.*

Pulse is the expansion and contraction of an artery, in rhythm with the heartbeat; it can be felt at various points on the body. Pulse rate varies with age, physical condition, emotional state, and level of activity. A baby's pulse may be as high as 120 to 140 beats per minute, whereas a resting adult's pulse may average about 70 to 72 beats per minute. A well-conditioned athlete may have a resting pulse of 50 to 60 beats per minute and a rate of up to 180 beats per minute when exercising strenuously. Pulse rate generally rises with a fever.

Irregularities in pulse, such as missed beats, can occur in healthy people but most often affect individuals who smoke or have some type of heart disease. Rapid pulse rate is called *tachycardia;* slow pulse rate is known as *bradycardia.*

Taking the Pulse   The pulse can be measured wherever an artery lies across a bone. It is usually taken at the wrist by placing two or three fingers (not the thumb) lightly just below the base of the thumb where the beats of the pulse through the *radial artery* can be felt. Count the number of beats during 1 full minute by using a watch or clock with a second hand, or count for 15 seconds and multiply by 4 (see illustration: Taking a Pulse).

The pulse can also be taken in the *carotid artery,* which is located on either side of the neck. (See also BLEEDING; CIRCULATORY SYSTEM, **1**.)

▶ RADIATION

Radiation refers to several kinds of invisible energy, some occurring naturally in the environment and others created by humans. Most often the term refers to *ionizing radiation,* a form of energy that produces electrically charged particles called *ions* in the molecules it strikes. Sources of ionizing radiation include cosmic rays, radioactivity, and X rays. *Nonionizing radiation,* the other major type, causes atoms to move within the objects it strikes, but does not produce ions. Common sources of nonionizing radiation are microwaves and magnetic fields.

Radiation has played an important part in the advancement of industrial and medical technology, but there are health concerns linked to radiation exposure. The risks related to ionizing radiation exposure are the best documented. Overexposure to this type of radiation can lead to cancer, immune system damage, and birth defects.

Sources and Health Risks of Ionizing Radiation   Small amounts of ionizing radiation form a natural part of the earth's environment. Everyone is exposed to radiation from cosmic rays that come from both the sun and the outer universe. Another source of natural radiation is rocks or soil that contain radioactive mineral deposits, which emit ionizing radiation as the radioactive material decays. A third common source of ionizing radiation is RADON gas. Ionizing radiation is emitted in the form of alpha particles, beta particles, and gamma rays. *Gamma rays* penetrate most deeply into the body and pose the greatest threat to health.

Human activity has generated additional sources of ionizing radiation. A common source is medical X rays, which account for about 11 percent of the average person's yearly exposure to radiation. Nuclear reactors, which harness the energy of nuclear fission to produce electrical power, also produce ionizing radiation. This radiation is normally contained by huge shields, but it is potentially harmful if it leaks out as the result of a nuclear accident. The radioactive wastes produced by reactors are another potential danger because there are no completely safe ways to store or dispose of them. Last, the threat of mass exposure to ionizing radiation is one of the many great risks associated with the manufacture, storage, testing, and use of nuclear weapons. (See also NUCLEAR POWER.)

Sources and Health Risks of Nonionizing Radiation   Nonionizing radiation comes from a number of natural and artificial sources. One natural source is ultraviolet (UV) light from the sun. Most UV radiation is absorbed by the OZONE layer in the atmosphere. Certain pollutants, however, are depleting the ozone layer, which is allowing more UV rays to reach the earth. Higher levels of UV radiation pose many potential health threats to humans, including increased risk of *skin cancer* and damage to the immune system.

Another type of nonionizing radiation is *electromagnetic radiation*. This comes from a variety of human-made sources, including microwave ovens, televisions, and the visual display terminals, or VDTs, that are used with computers. Several high-tech medical devices, including ultrasound and *magnetic resonance imaging* (MRI) equipment, also emit nonionizing radiation. Another source of electromagnetic radiation is the magnetic fields that exist around the wires that carry electricity. Strong fields are produced by electric power stations and high-voltage power lines; relatively weak fields surround other power lines and even household wiring and appliances.

The hazards of electromagnetic radiation are still being debated. Although some studies have shown a statistical correlation between exposure to high levels of this radiation and birth defects or certain types of cancer, scientists are unsure how such radiation could cause damage. Some experts discount any possible risk; others urge individuals to limit their exposure to this type of radiation whenever possible.

Working with Radiation.
Workers who handle radioactive materials such as uranium take many precautions to limit their exposure to radiation.

HEALTHY CHOICES
●●●●●●●●●●●●

Limiting Radiation Exposure   Experts suggest a number of ways that people can limit their exposure to potentially harmful radiation. Limiting the time spent in the sun and using sun-block products can limit exposure to UV radiation. Today's X-ray equipment is safer than ever before, but X rays should be used only when necessary. Pregnant women should not have X-ray examinations unless special precautions are taken.

Governments work to make sure that nuclear reactors are safe and that nuclear waste is disposed of as carefully as possible. Many of the nations of the world are working together to reduce the manufacture and stockpiling of nuclear weapons. (See also HAZARDOUS WASTE; SUN DAMAGE; CANCER, 3; MAGNETIC RESONANCE IMAGING, 3; RADIATION THERAPY, 3; SKIN CANCER, 3; X-RAY EXAMINATION, 3.)

▶ RADON

Measuring Radon Levels. *The two most popular devices for measuring radon levels are an activated-charcoal detector and the alpha-track detector. The alpha-track detector measures levels over a period of months.*

Radon is a colorless, odorless radioactive gas produced by the decay of uranium. It occurs naturally in certain soils, rocks, and groundwater. It is also emitted by building materials made from these soils or rocks. Although radon is harmless in the open air, it can reach dangerous levels in enclosed spaces such as the interiors of well-insulated homes and other buildings. Recent studies suggest that prolonged exposure to high concentrations of radon can greatly increase a person's risk of developing lung cancer. In fact, the Environmental Protection Agency estimates that 20,000 of the 130,000 annual lung-cancer deaths are the result of exposure to radon.

In most cases, radon enters a building from the surrounding soil by seeping in through cracks and other openings in the foundation. The concentration of radon in indoor air depends on the amount of uranium found in the ground (or building material), the permeability of the soil, and the air flow within the structure itself. In enclosed spaces, especially basements, radon may attach itself to particles of dust floating freely in the air. When inhaled, these particles lodge themselves in the lungs, where they release low levels of RADIATION. Over a period of years, this exposure can damage the lungs, increasing a person's risk of cancer. The combination of radon exposure and cigarette smoking is particularly lethal. (See also LUNG CANCER, 3.)

A number of devices are available to measure radon levels within the home. If levels are high, minor modifications may be necessary. These may include sealing cracks and other openings in basement floors and walls and installing special ventilation systems.

▶ RECYCLING

Recycling is the recovery and reuse of waste materials for other purposes or in other products. It is one of the three basic principles of environmentally sound WASTE MANAGEMENT—reducing the amount of waste, reusing rather than throwing out, and recycling. Putting these ideas into practice can help conserve natural resources, reduce the amount of waste that needs to be disposed of, and reduce the pollution that may result from the disposal of waste materials. In terms of its impact on the environment

Recycling Centers. *At a recycling center, materials are first sorted so that they can be melted down and used to make new products.*

and on the consumption of limited resources, recycling is one of the most effective ways of dealing with waste.

Recycling Methods   There are several methods of recycling. One involves using waste materials produced in industry and agriculture for other purposes. For example, waste materials produced in manufacturing processes can be burned to make steam or electricity, and ash residue can be used in building roads and in making concrete. In agriculture, plant and animal wastes can be *composted,* that is, broken down naturally by the action of air and microorganisms. The resulting substance can be used to nourish plants.

Another method of recycling involves using waste materials in the manufacture of new products. Glass and metal waste, for example, can be melted down and then used to make new glass or metal products. Newspapers from which the ink has been removed can be made into recycled paper products.

Reusing materials or products for their original purpose is another form of recycling. Returnable bottles, for example, can be reused over and over again.

Savings from Recycling   In addition to conserving resources and protecting the environment, recycling can often save money. Extracting raw materials for use in industry requires large amounts of energy. Recycling requires less energy and therefore lowers costs. For example, it takes about 20 times as much energy to produce a ton of aluminum from newly mined ore as it does to produce a ton of aluminum from scrap metal. Such energy savings can be an economic incentive for recycling. Savings can also result from decreased cost of pollution cleanup and decreased use of natural resources. Another possible economic benefit of recycling is the creation of thousands of new jobs. Many more people are employed in recycling processes than in running incinerators and landfills, for example.

The Future of Recycling   The U.S. Environmental Protection Agency (EPA) set as a goal for 1992 that households should recycle 25 percent of their waste. This goal was not met, but progress is being made. Today many communities have established recycling centers for the collection of recyclables. The success of community programs will depend on the motivation and responsibility of individuals as well as on continued markets for recycled materials.

Today, industries are recycling more and more of their waste materials. As energy and raw materials become more expensive in the future, industries will have even greater incentive to recycle.

HEALTHY CHOICES

To encourage recycling, new technologies are needed to make recycling easier and more cost-effective. This might include more efficient ways of recovering metals and other substances from waste material, new methods of producing energy from waste, and better procedures for separating recyclable materials from nonrecyclable waste. People can help in recycling efforts by participating in existing recycling programs, buying recycled goods, buying durable products designed for reuse and repair rather than disposable ones, and reusing products as much as possible. (See also SOLID WASTE.)

▶ RICE

RICE stands for simple first-aid procedures for many minor sports-related INJURIES, such as sprains and strains. The letters stand for Rest, Ice, Compression, and Elevation.

Rest   Resting the injured body part reduces pain, prevents aggravating the injury, and promotes healing.

Ice   An injury should be cooled as soon as possible to help reduce pain and decrease swelling. Applying cold slows blood flow, which reduces internal bleeding and swelling. This in turn helps limit damage to tissue and thereby speeds healing. Use a commercial ice pack or place ice cubes or crushed ice in a plastic bag or hot water bottle. Wrap the ice pack in a thick towel, apply it to the injured area, and leave the ice in place for 10 to 20 minutes. Reapply every 2 hours during waking hours for the next 2

RICE.   *Rest, ice, compression and elevation are four steps that are useful in treating minor sports-related injuries.*

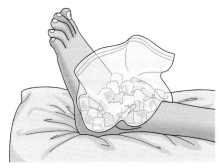

Ice. Applying cold to an injury helps reduce pain and swelling.

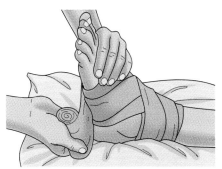

Compression. Wrapping an injury firmly helps keep down swelling by preventing excess fluids from gathering in the injured tissues.

days. Do not apply ice for longer than 20 minutes at a time because skin or nerve damage may result.

Compression   Compressing the injured area helps prevent excess fluids from accumulating in tissues. Wrap the injury firmly with an elastic bandage or a towel, but do not cut off circulation to the area.

Elevation   Raising the injured area above the level of the heart helps prevent excess fluids from accumulating in the tissues. At night this is especially important because the body remains immobile for many hours.

CONSULT A PHYSICIAN

Further Treatment   If an injury shows no improvement after using the RICE procedures for 48 hours, see a physician. Severe injuries always require professional treatment, including special exercises prescribed by a sports physician or physical therapist. (See also FIRST AID; SPORTS INJURIES, 4.)

▶ **SAFETY BELTS**   see AUTOMOBILE SAFETY

▶ **SAFETY EQUIPMENT**   Safety equipment is any type of device or clothing that helps prevent ACCIDENTS and INJURIES. Safety equipment can be as elaborate as the suits worn by workers who handle hazardous substances or as simple as the pads and gloves worn by skateboarders. Having and using the right safety equipment plays an important role in protecting health on the job, at home, and in many activities.

Most safety equipment provides active protection, passive protection, or some elements of both. Active protection includes devices that the user is responsible for employing, such as safety helmets and goggles. Passive devices, on the other hand, provide protection with little or no effort from the user. Examples of passive devices include automatic shut-off switches on machinery and household smoke detectors. For any type of safety equipment to be effective, it must be used in a proper manner and kept in good condition. The equipment that is purchased and installed should meet the generally accepted safety standards for its intended use.

Safety Equipment in the Home   Fire is a leading cause of injury in the home. Therefore, among the most important articles of home safety equipment are smoke detectors and fire extinguishers. When properly installed and maintained, *smoke detectors* alert people to fire and provide enough warning to save lives. Smoke detectors must be tested periodically to see that they still work. In some cases, the batteries may have to be replaced or new detectors installed. *Fire extinguishers* come in several types, each effective against a certain type of fire, such as a grease fire or an electrical fire. Extinguishers should be placed in areas where they are likely to be used and checked frequently. The type purchased should be easy to use.

Workplace Safety. *Hard hats are important on construction sites because of the danger of falling objects. A hard hat will help protect the head from serious injury.*

Other home safety devices can help prevent such accidents as ELECTRIC SHOCK, POISONING, or falls. Installing a ground fault circuit interrupter (GFCI) on an outlet or a circuit breaker can prevent severe or fatal accidents with electrical appliances. In homes with small children, childproof latches can help prevent children from opening cupboards with household poisons or medications or opening a basement door. (See also ELECTRICAL SAFETY; FIRE SAFETY; HOME SAFETY.)

Safety Equipment in the Workplace   Many jobs involve hazards that can cause serious injury or death. These workplaces are required by law to provide safety equipment to protect workers. Special glasses or goggles and face masks are used to protect the eyes, nose, and throat against exposure to irritating fumes or particles in the air. In places with a high noise level, specially designed ear protectors such as earmuffs or earplugs can effectively reduce the risk of damage to hearing. Work gloves can help prevent hand injuries or irritation in some workplaces. At construction sites or other places where falling objects are a hazard, hard hats are an important safeguard against serious head injury. (See also NOISE POLLUTION; HEARING LOSS, **3.**)

In addition to safety equipment that is worn, most machinery has built-in safety devices that can help reduce the risk of injury. Meat slicing equipment and farm machinery, for example, usually offer such protection.

Safety Equipment in a Vehicle   Motor vehicles are equipped with many safety features designed to help avoid accidents or protect passengers from serious injury in a collision. Among the most important protection devices are seat belts, air bags, and specially designed car seats for children. Wearing a lap and shoulder belt reduces the chance of injury or death in an accident by nearly 60 percent. An air bag in conjunction with a seat belt can reduce this risk even further, particularly in a head-on collision. For small children—among whom the leading cause of death is automobile accidents—using a car seat greatly reduces the risk of serious harm. (See also AUTOMOBILE SAFETY.)

Safety Equipment for Recreation   Many sports and recreation activities involve the chance of accident and injury. Using the appropriate protective gear is a simple precaution that can reduce the risk of the most common types of injuries. Head injuries are among the most common and serious of bicycling injuries; the use of a well-designed, properly fitted helmet can greatly reduce this risk. Bicyclists riding at night should wear reflective material on clothes and have headlights and taillights to alert drivers to their presence on the road. (See also BICYCLE SAFETY.)

For sports like squash and racquetball, shatterproof eyewear can help shield the eyes from injury. For boating activities, life vests or other types of flotation devices are essential. They are also important for young children swimming in pools, lakes, or the ocean. (See also WATER SAFETY.)

SAFETY ON THE JOB

RISK FACTORS
▶ ▶ ▶ ▶ ▶ ▶

Job safety is a major public health concern in the United States. Each year as many as 10,000 people are killed in ACCIDENTS on the job, and millions experience job-related illnesses and INJURIES. Workers are most likely to die or suffer injuries in agriculture, construction, mining, forestry, fishing, transportation, and manufacturing occupations.

More than one-third of all fatalities on the job involve motor vehicles. Other fatal work accidents involve falls, BURNS, ELECTRIC SHOCK, suffocation, and POISONING. Occupational injuries and illnesses include lung diseases caused by inhaling TOXIC SUBSTANCES such as cotton dust, ASBESTOS, metal particles, silica dust, coal dust, and cancer-causing chemicals. (See also PARTICULATES.)

Other common kinds of injuries include hearing loss and repetitive motion injuries. Many factory workers suffer hearing loss from NOISE POLLUTION, caused by such things as loud machinery or airplane engines.

Hearing Protection. *Workers in this factory wear special ear protection because of the high level of noise on the factory floor.*

Workers who use their hands to perform repetitive tasks like keyboarding or assembly-line work may develop pain in arms, wrists, or neck. (See also CARPAL TUNNEL SYNDROME, **3**.)

Preventing Injuries and Illness Employers and government agencies can improve safety on the job in a number of ways. Methods include active and passive prevention measures. Active prevention measures require workers to take specific actions to prevent accidents. These include using safety belts and other SAFETY EQUIPMENT, such as hard hats and ear plugs, and handling and storing hazardous materials properly. Passive prevention measures require no action by workers. These include built-in safety switches, air bags, and air ventilation systems that filter harmful substances out of the air.

Many industries also provide training in safety procedures to reduce injuries. State and federal laws require employers to meet minimum safety standards to help protect workers. These may require such things as the installation of sprinkler systems or the providing of protective masks and equipment for working around harmful substances. (See also OCCUPATIONAL SAFETY AND HEALTH ADMINISTRATION.)

▶ SANITATION

Sanitation involves efforts to control the physical environment in order to prevent disease and promote health. Many sanitation efforts occur on the federal, state, or local level through public health agencies. Sanitation also involves individual decisions that people make in their homes. Proper sanitation can help ensure a clean environment and significantly reduce the incidence of disease.

The History of Sanitation Centuries ago, a lack of adequate sanitation caused unhealthy living conditions that often contributed to the spread of disease. Catastrophic outbreaks of diseases like cholera and bubonic plague could be attributed directly to unsanitary conditions. During the nineteenth and twentieth centuries, efforts to purify drinking water, dispose of SEWAGE, inspect food supplies, and control disease-carrying insects have greatly reduced the incidence of disease in developed areas of the world.

Public Sanitation Efforts In the United States, sanitation efforts help protect the health of the community. These efforts include the design and management of water and sewage treatment plants; the supervision of food processing, handling, and distribution; and the disposal of solid wastes. Such activities help guarantee that water supplies are pure and contain no bacteria or other pathogens (disease-causing microorganisms) and that food is not contaminated by pathogens or chemical poisons. Public health measures are also aimed at eliminating disease-carrying insects and rodents and ensuring the cleanliness and safety of public buildings such as hotels, restaurants, and office buildings. Most communities have regulations requiring factories, hospitals, restaurants, and other public facilities to meet certain sanitation standards. Places that fail to meet these standards can be fined and forced to take steps to comply with regulations.

Restaurant Sanitation. *Restaurants have strict standards that apply to people who handle food. These may include wearing gloves and special head coverings and frequent handwashing.*

Home Sanitation and Safety   In addition to public sanitation efforts, much can be done within the home to ensure a safe environment. Sanitation in the home means keeping bacteria out of food through personal cleanliness and proper food handling procedures. It also means maintaining a clean environment. Methods to ensure *food safety* include washing hands before handling food, keeping utensils and preparation surfaces clean, and cooking and storing foods at the proper temperatures. Following such procedures can help prevent poisoning or illness caused by bacterial contamination. (See also FOOD SAFETY, 4.)

The destruction of organisms that cause infection or disease is called *antisepsis.* In addition to personal cleanliness and proper food handling, antisepsis can also be achieved through the use of antiseptics and disinfectants. *Antiseptics,* which are substances that destroy germs on living tissue, can be applied to the skin and mucous membranes to help prevent infection entering the body through cuts or scratches. *Disinfectants,* which are substances that can destroy germs on nonliving objects, can help sanitize clothes, rooms, household surfaces, and utensils. Maintaining sanitary conditions at home and in public places can help prevent the spread of disease. (See also HOME SAFETY; WATER POLLUTION; COMMUNICABLE DISEASE, 2; INFECTION, 2; ANTISEPTICS, 7.)

▶ SEWAGE

Sewage, also called wastewater, is liquid that contains human and animal waste and waste materials produced by industry and other human activities. Sewage contains both dissolved substances, such as chemicals and detergents, and pieces of solid matter, such as human feces and bits of garbage. It usually also contains bacteria, viruses, and other organisms that, along with harmful chemicals, can damage health or cause disease. Because most sewage eventually flows into rivers, lakes, and oceans, it

Sewage Treatment Plants. At sewage treatment plants like this one, human and industrial wastes are processed. Treated liquid is returned to the environment.

can contaminate water supplies and harm wildlife unless it is treated and disposed of properly.

Sewage Treatment Processes   The basic process for treating sewage involves removing the solid waste materials and treating the remaining liquid before releasing it into the environment. In cities and many towns, pipes carry untreated sewage to special treatment plants where the solid materials are filtered out. This material can sometimes be used as a fertilizer. The remaining liquid, called *effluent,* is treated to destroy harmful bacteria and then released into waterways. Some systems treat the effluent several times to destroy as many harmful substances as possible before release.

Homes in rural areas may have *septic tanks,* which are large underground tanks to hold sewage, and *leaching fields,* which consist of a series of buried pipes with openings. As sewage enters the septic tank, solid materials sink to the bottom, and the effluent flows out into the leaching field. Bacteria in the septic tank change the solids into a gas and a less harmful substance called humus that is pumped out periodically and disposed of. As the effluent passes through the leaching field, bacteria in the soil help destroy harmful substances.

Sewage Disposal Problems   Many sewage systems today do not do an adequate job of treating sewage and protecting human health and the environment. Some systems are aging and inefficient. Others are too small to accommodate growing populations and the increased use of water in industry and households. And most are not able to remove certain toxic chemicals. As a result, sewage remains a problem for health and the environment despite the progress that has been made in treatment and disposal during the past few decades. (See also SANITATION; WASTE MANAGEMENT; WATER POLLUTION; WATER PURITY.)

SMOG

Photochemical Smog. *When automobile exhaust gases mix with oxygen and sunlight, photochemical smog is formed. In a city like Los Angeles, which lies in a basin, the pollutants in smog can reach dangerous levels.*

Smog is the visible AIR POLLUTION that sometimes hangs over major cities. The term *smog* was originally created to describe a mixture of smoke and fog, but it now refers to any visible combination of airborne pollutants. These may include smoke, ashes, soot, metals, and sulphur and nitrogen oxides. There are two kinds of smog. One is gray or *industrial smog,* caused by the burning of FOSSIL FUELS. Industrial smog is common in cities like London and New York. Brown or *photochemical smog,* caused mainly by the reaction of sunlight and oxygen with exhaust gases from vehicles, is more typical of cities like Los Angeles and Mexico City that lie in basins, areas surrounded by higher land.

Smog can reach dangerous levels when it becomes trapped beneath a layer of warm air. Even mild smog can cause burning in the eyes, nose, and throat and damage plant life. Severe smog can be fatal for people with heart diseases and respiratory illnesses. Although emission-control devices on automobiles and industrial smokestacks reduce the pollutants that cause smog, it remains a major problem in many cities around the world. (See also ACID RAIN; OZONE; PARTICULATES; TEMPERATURE INVERSION.)

▷ **SMOKE DETECTORS** see FIRE SAFETY

▷ **SMOKE INHALATION**   Smoke inhalation occurs when smoke, which includes carbon monoxide and other TOXIC SUBSTANCES, is breathed into the airways and lungs. This is a deadly danger during fires, when flammable materials such as wood, plastics, and chemicals produce smoke that contains solid particles or toxic fumes. Smoke inhalation is frequently the actual cause of death in a fire.

Treatment for Smoke Inhalation. *Emergency personnel routinely give oxygen at the scene of the fire to people who have inhaled smoke and fumes.*

Symptoms and Complications   A victim of smoke inhalation may gasp for breath, cough, or choke. Other symptoms are irritated eyes, singed nasal hairs, or gurgling sounds when breathing. Inhaled smoke can cause respiratory-tract damage such as a buildup of fluid in the lungs as well as unconsciousness or death from asphyxiation.

First Aid   It is important for a person experiencing smoke inhalation to be moved to a smoke-free area as soon as possible. If it is necessary to enter a smoke-filled area to rescue the person, keep low to the floor. If smoke is dense, let professional rescue personnel handle the situation. The victim's breathing and heartbeat should be monitored; if necessary, artificial respiration or CPR (cardiopulmonary resuscitation) can be administered by a trained person.

Call for emergency medical assistance immediately, even if the person seems to have recovered. Cases of severe smoke inhalation may require hospitalization to administer oxygen, intravenous fluids, or drugs to widen airways to the lungs. Treatment for shock may also be needed.

Preventing Smoke Inhalation   During a fire, remain calm and follow FIRE SAFETY guidelines. Leave a burning building quickly, and call for help from a neighboring building. Avoid breathing smoke by staying close to the floor, where concentrations of smoke will be less dense. If trapped in a room by a fire, shut the door and block any cracks around it with blankets, pillows, or other material to prevent smoke from entering the room. Then go to a window and shout for help. (See also BURNS; FIRST AID; SHOCK, **3.**)

▷ **SOLAR ENERGY**   Solar energy is the energy that is produced by the sun. The solar energy that radiates to earth provides the light and warmth that make it possible for all life to exist here. It also produces the weather patterns that determine the earth's climate.

Solar energy reaches the earth in the form of solar RADIATION. The amount of radiation that strikes the earth in an hour is greater than all the energy produced on earth in an entire year. Although solar radiation is clean, free, and a renewable form of energy, it is difficult and expensive to capture and is distributed unequally around the world.

Solar Heating. *Rooftop collectors convert the sun's energy into heat that can be used in the home.*

Uses of Solar Energy Solar energy has long been used in warm, sunny climates to heat homes and produce hot water. In the 1970s, when a fuel shortage made gas and oil expensive, the U.S. government financed research to develop solar energy techniques along with other forms of alternative energy. This research led to improvements in solar energy collection units, making it practical to use them in homes and buildings even in moderate climates.

Many newer homes are designed with *passive solar heating systems* that use the orientation and architecture of the building to collect solar energy. A passive system uses slanted windows, special roofing materials, insulation, and ventilation systems to trap the sun's heat to warm rooms and control sunlight.

Some contemporary buildings include *active solar energy systems* that use pumps to transfer solar heat collected in special panels to hot water tanks or radiators. The solar panels have black heat-absorbing surfaces. Water passing through the tubes attached to the panels is heated and then carried to storage tanks for later use. Although a solar system cannot provide all the energy needs of a house or office building in a cold climate, it can reduce the consumption of FOSSIL FUELS.

Solar energy systems can also generate other kinds of power. Some industries use solar energy to generate electricity or produce steam to drive electric generators or turbines. Solar furnaces are special devices that can generate temperatures of 5000°F (3000°C). Solar batteries power some watches and calculators, but they are not efficient enough for larger appliances because sunlight is so diffuse on earth. In space, however, solar batteries can collect direct sunlight and generate enough energy to power satellites.

Future of Solar Energy Although solar energy is free, the machinery needed to capture and circulate it remains expensive. In hot, sunny countries, such as those around the Mediterranean Sea, rooftop solar collectors are already a cheap, practical means of heating homes and providing hot water. Many countries, including the United States, are experimenting with solar fields, gigantic solar collectors that can generate large amounts of electrical power for commercial use. As technology continues to improve and sources of fossil fuel become more scarce, it is likely that solar energy will become an increasingly important fuel source in the future.

SOLID WASTE

Solid waste is any kind of nonliquid refuse or trash. Solid waste includes such things as waste paper, food, glass, plastic, and metal; junked automobiles, tires, appliances, and furniture; and some agricultural and industrial wastes. The quantity of solid waste has increased dramatically in recent decades as a result of POPULATION GROWTH and the increased production of consumer goods. In the United States alone, nearly a billion pounds of solid wastes are disposed of each day. This growing mountain of trash threatens to blight the landscape and perhaps adversely affect human health and the environment.

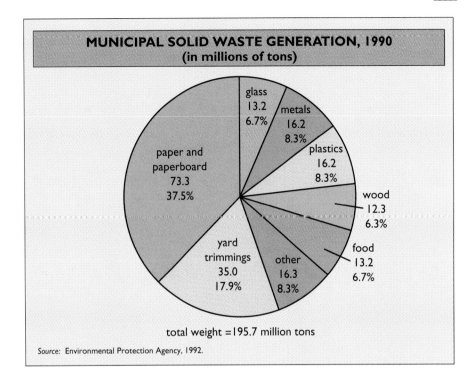

MUNICIPAL SOLID WASTE GENERATION, 1990
(in millions of tons)

glass
13.2
6.7%

metals
16.2
8.3%

plastics
16.2
8.3%

wood
12.3
6.3%

food
13.2
6.7%

paper and
paperboard
73.3
37.5%

yard
trimmings
35.0
17.9%

other
16.3
8.3%

total weight =195.7 million tons

Source: Environmental Protection Agency, 1992.

Disposing of Solid Waste For many years, solid wastes were simply thrown away in open dumps, burned in open containers, or dropped in the oceans. Little attention was paid to how these disposal methods might affect the environment or human health. In some instances, solid waste is still disposed of in such ways. Some cities, for example, still use *ocean dumping* as a method of solid waste disposal, and open garbage dumps and uncontrolled burning still exist in some rural areas. Greater health and environmental awareness, however, has led to more controlled methods of solid waste disposal, although there are still problems involved.

Today, much solid waste is disposed of in sanitary *landfills.* These are specially planned and supervised disposal sites in which waste is disposed of in pits. The waste is deposited in layers, compacted to reduce its volume, and then covered with soil. Alternating layers of solid waste and soil helps encourage decomposition, reduce unpleasant odors, and keep animals away. Sanitary landfills have some drawbacks, however. Harmful substances may seep into the ground and contaminate soil or water. Moreover, available space for sanitary landfills is becoming increasingly scarce.

Another method of solid waste disposal is *incineration,* or burning in specially designed furnaces. Incinerated materials are converted to gases by burning them at very high temperatures, leaving a small amount of residue that is usually disposed of in landfills. In addition to reducing the volume of solid waste, incineration can also be used to create steam for use in heating or to generate electricity. Unfortunately, incineration may also contribute to AIR POLLUTION.

Reducing Solid Waste The ability to deal with the growing volume of solid waste will depend in part on reducing solid waste at its source and on RECYCLING. Reducing solid waste at its source involves both manufacturers and consumers in making and buying products with less packaging, that are reusable, or that are *biodegradable*—that decompose naturally in the environment. Recycling is becoming an increasingly popular means of reducing the volume of solid waste. To be most effective, however, it requires planning, ample markets for recycled materials, community or government support, and active participation by individuals. (See also SANITATION.)

▶ SPOUSE ABUSE

Spouse abuse is the physical or emotional mistreatment of one spouse by the other. Physical abuse may involve hitting or kicking whereas emotional abuse may include abusive ridicule and harsh criticism. In the great majority of cases, the man is the abuser and the woman is the victim. An estimated 2 million women are victims of spouse abuse in the United States each year, compared with roughly 250,000 men.

Spouse abuse is probably the most underreported crime in the United States. Until recently, judges and police, as well as society in general, tended to tolerate spouse abuse as a private family matter, even though the same behavior directed at a stranger would be a crime. These attitudes are changing, however, and law enforcement agencies are becoming more willing to arrest and prosecute abusive spouses.

Spouse Abuse. *Some kinds of abuse are not as evident as physical abuse, as when one spouse is emotionally abusive toward the other.*

The Abuse Cycle   People who are abused or who witness spouse abuse as children tend to become abusive adults or the victims of abuse. They grow up believing that such abuse is a normal part of family life. Stress, such as unemployment, poverty, debt, and job dissatisfaction, can often trigger spouse abuse. Once a pattern of abuse is established, it usually continues and escalates. Often the abuse ends in HOMICIDE; more than 40 percent of all female murder victims are killed by their husbands, and more than 10 percent of male murder victims are killed by their wives.

Intervention   Help for the abused spouse is sometimes hard to find. Protection from the courts has been largely unsuccessful. *Restraining orders*, court orders barring the violent spouse from having any contact with the abused partner, are sometimes used. Statistics indicate, however, that the threat of arrest frequently does nothing to curb abusive behavior. A number of experts believe that the best way to deal with spouse abuse is to leave the abusive situation, but many victims of abuse find this difficult. Some are unable to leave because they are emotionally tied to the abuser, others because they don't have the financial resources to leave, especially if they have small children. In some parts of the country, social service agencies operate shelters for abused spouses. Support groups and counseling for both abusers and their victims can also be helpful and are available in many localities. (See also CHILD ABUSE; VIOLENCE.)

▶ SPRAINS AND STRAINS

Sprains and strains are common injuries that occur when joints, muscles, or ligaments are twisted or stretched beyond their normal range of motion. Strains involve muscles; sprains involve joints and ligaments.

Strains, also called muscle pulls, occur when muscles are stretched too far and their fibers begin to tear. Symptoms include pain and tenderness, rapid swelling, and impaired muscle function. Strains can occur when lifting a heavy weight or with sudden movements, such as stretching to catch a football. They are most common in the muscles of the back, thigh, groin, and shoulder.

Sprains occur when sudden force, often a twisting movement, damages *ligaments,* the bands that hold the joints in position (see illustration: When a Sprain Occurs). Sprains range from minor tears to complete ruptures of the ligaments. Symptoms include painful swelling of the joint, pain when the joint is moved, discoloration of the tissues, and spasms of the surrounding muscles. The ankle is most vulnerable to sprains because it must support the weight of the body. The knee, which must absorb twisting stresses when the body rotates from the hips, is also frequently injured by sprains.

First Aid for Sprains and Strains   Minor injuries can be helped with RICE, which stands for rest, ice, compression, and elevation. Resting the injured body part helps promote healing and prevent further injury. Applying ice helps decrease swelling, pain, and muscle spasms. Compressing the *injured area* with an elastic bandage and elevating it above the level of the heart will also help reduce swelling. Aspirin or another analgesic will relieve pain. (See also ANALGESICS, 7.)

CONSULT A
PHYSICIAN

Serious strains and sprains should be treated by a physician. Symptoms of serious injury include a popping sound when the injury occurs, loss of feeling in the affected area, immediate difficulty in using the joint, and pain and impaired movement lasting for more than 2 or 3 days. A physician may order an X-ray examination to look for a FRACTURE. Sprains and strains may be treated with anti-inflammatory drugs; severe injuries may require surgical repair.

RISK FACTORS
► ► ► ► ► ►
HEALTHY CHOICES
• • • • • • • • • • •

Preventing Strains and Sprains   The risk of strains increases when muscles have not been warmed up before participating in a sport or activity. Stretching all the muscles that will be used or slowly performing the movement of the sport or exercise can help prevent strains. Jogging in place for 5 minutes or stationary cycling for 5 to 10 minutes increases blood flow to the area and warms the muscles gradually.

When a Sprain Occurs.   *The ankle is a common site for sprains. In a sprain, the ligaments that support the joint are damaged.*

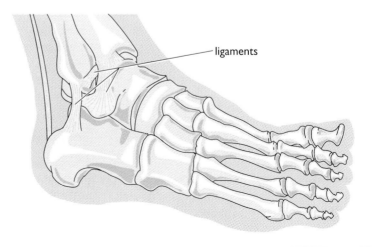

ligaments

SAFETY AND ENVIRONMENTAL HEALTH

The best safeguard against sprains is strong, flexible muscles. Stretching the calf muscles and strengthening the muscles that surround the ankles helps prevent ankle sprains. Knee sprains can be minimized by strengthening the quadriceps, the muscles along the front of the thigh. (See also DISLOCATIONS; ANKLE, 1; CONNECTIVE TISSUE, 1; KNEE, 1; MUSCLE, 1.)

▶ ## STINGS

see BITES AND STINGS

▶ ## SUN DAMAGE

Protecting the Skin. *A sunscreen as well as a sun block on the more sensitive areas of the face can help protect against the damaging effects of the sun.*

RISK FACTORS
▶ ▶ ▶ ▶ ▶ ▶

Sun damage is any injury to the skin caused by exposure to ultraviolet (UV) RADIATION from the sun. Short-term exposure may result in sunburn, an inflammation of the skin characterized by redness, pain, and itching. Recurrent exposure may lead to skin discoloration, premature aging of the skin, and skin cancer. Studies suggest that people who receive severe, blistering sunburns when they are young are particularly likely to develop skin cancer later in life.

Sunburn The most common form of sun damage is sunburn. In mild cases, the skin becomes red and tender. Several days after the burning, the dead skin cells peel and flake away. In more severe cases, the skin may become inflamed and form painful blisters. People suffering from severe sunburn may also experience headaches, dizziness, fever, vomiting, and shock. Another, though less serious, complication of severe sunburn is an itchy rash known as *sun poisoning.* Repeated bouts of sunburn can cause the skin to *prematurely age* by becoming yellowed and wrinkled, encourage the growth of warty lumps known as *keratoses,* and increase a person's risk of developing skin cancer.

Sunburn occurs most often in those with fair skin. Fair-skinned people have less of the light-absorbing *melanin* pigment than do dark-skinned people and are consequently more vulnerable to the harmful effects of ultraviolet radiation. In addition, people taking certain medications, such as birth-control pills, antidepressants, and antibiotics, are more likely to experience adverse reactions to sunlight.

Many people visit tanning salons in an effort to acquire what they believe is a safe, painless tan. The longer-wave ultraviolet light used at most tanning salons, however, actually penetrates the skin more deeply than does the radiation absorbed by sunbathers. Even though tanning treatments may not burn the outer layers of the skin, they can damage underlying blood vessels. Like natural suntans, they can also cause premature aging of the skin.

Treatment and Prevention A person with a sunburn should move to a shady area immediately. The burned skin should then be immersed in cool water or cooled with an ice pack. Calamine lotion may be applied to provide relief, and aspirin or other anti-inflammatory medications help to reduce pain and swelling. Blisters should be left to heal naturally. If they break open accidentally, an antibacterial ointment should be applied to prevent infection. If a person has a severe burn or develops other symptoms, a physician should be contacted.

Everyone can take steps to prevent the harmful effects of sunlight. Fair-skinned people who expect to spend a long period of time outside should wear protective clothing and a sunscreen. Clothing should include a long-sleeved shirt of tightly woven material, long pants, and a hat. High-quality *sunscreens* contain at least two UV-light–absorbing ingredients, such as para-aminobenzoic acid (PABA) or benzophenone. Most people should choose a sunscreen with a Sun Protection Factor (SPF) of at least 15. Liberal amounts should be applied to the skin at least 30 minutes before exposure to the sun and reapplied at regular intervals. In addition, because the sun's ultraviolet radiation is most intense between the hours of 10 A.M. and 3 P.M., outdoor activities should be scheduled for early in the morning or late in the afternoon. (See also HEATSTROKE; OZONE; SKIN CANCER, 3; SUNSCREENS, 7.)

► ## SUPERFUND

Superfund is the unofficial name for a federal program administered by the U.S. Environmental Protection Agency (EPA) to clean up toxic waste dump sites. Passed by Congress in 1980, the Superfund act empowers the EPA to bring lawsuits against the companies and individuals responsible for creating toxic waste dumps—including site owners, waste generators, and transporters—to recover the costs of cleaning up the sites. The act also established the National Priority List (NPL) of those sites considered the most dangerous and therefore earmarked for the earliest action.

The Superfund program was renewed in 1986 and also in 1991. However, many environmentalists have been disappointed with its progress. By the early 1990s, Superfund had identified more than 1,200 sites in need of cleanup but had completed work on fewer than 30.

STATES WITH MOST NATIONAL PRIORITY LIST SITES, 1992			
State	**Final**	**Proposed**	**Total**
New Jersey	108	0	108
Pennsylvania	94	6	100
California	87	8	95
New York	83	1	84
Michigan	77	0	77
Florida	51	4	55
Washington	45	4	49
Minnesota	39	2	41
Wisconsin	39	1	40
Illinois	36	1	37

Source: Environmental Protection Agency.

ENVIRONMENTAL ORGANIZATIONS and other citizens' groups can petition the EPA and state environmental agencies to have a particular site placed on the NPL. Local citizens' groups often take an active role in monitoring the progress of the EPA in processing local sites for Superfund cleanup. They can read and comment on all studies and proposals and demand immediate action on any sites that pose a danger to human health or the environment. (See also TOXIC SUBSTANCES.)

▶ TEMPERATURE INVERSION

A temperature inversion, or thermal inversion, is a weather condition in which a layer of heavy, cool air becomes trapped beneath a layer of still, warm air. Normally, warm air lies closer to the earth with a layer of cooler air above. The natural rising of this warm air promotes air circulation and carries pollutants up and away. A temperature inversion, however, reverses this order. The warm upper layer acts as a lid to prevent the lower layer of air from moving. Certain land features increase the possibility of temperature inversions. For example, the city of Los Angeles, which lies in a valley surrounded by mountains and the ocean, has inversions 260 to 270 days each year.

RISK FACTORS
▶ ▶ ▶ ▶ ▶ ▶

A temperature inversion can be a serious health hazard when the trapped layer of air is full of pollutants. AIR POLLUTION levels increase dangerously because there is no way for the pollutants to be dispersed by winds or to rise higher in the atmosphere. Temperature inversions intensify any SMOG problem and increase the amount of OZONE in smog. During a temperature inversion, increased air pollution and ozone can have a dangerous impact on people's health, particularly among smokers, the elderly, and people with respiratory problems such as asthma.

Normal Conditions and a Temperature Inversion. *Under normal conditions, the warmest air lies closest to the earth. This air rises naturally, circulating the air and carrying pollutants up and away. During a temperature inversion, cool air near the ground is trapped under a layer of warm air. The warm layer acts as a lid, keeping stale, polluted air close to the ground.*

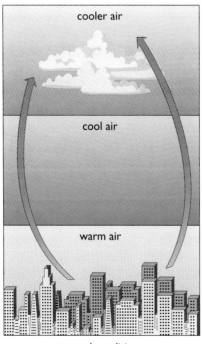

normal conditions

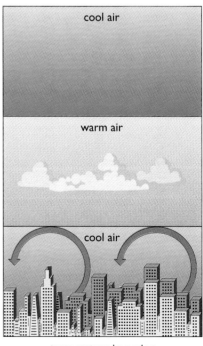

temperature inversion

There is little that can be done to prevent temperature inversions. However, attempts to improve air quality and reduce the amount of pollutants in the air can potentially make temperature inversions less of a threat to health.

▶ THERMAL POLLUTION

Thermal pollution is the discharge of hot water into lakes, streams, and oceans, disturbing the balance of the ECOSYSTEM. Even slight rises in temperature can interfere with the growth and reproduction of fish and plant life in natural systems. Rapid elevations of temperature can cause *thermal shock,* which can kill aquatic plants and animals. Thermal pollution also reduces the oxygen level in the water, inhibiting the water's ability to purify itself and support life.

The chief sources of thermal pollution are *industrial effluent,* or wastewater from factories, and water from power plant cooling systems that becomes heated when it is used to cool equipment or create steam. The federal government now recognizes warm water as a major pollutant and has begun to regulate thermal pollution. Companies can prevent thermal pollution by cooling wastewater in cooling towers before discharging it into waterways. (See also SEWAGE; WATER POLLUTION.)

▶ TOXIC SUBSTANCES

Toxic substances are chemicals that are present in air, water, or the food chain that cause harm to plants, animals, people, and the environment. In humans, toxic substances can cause many health problems, including sterility, birth defects, respiratory illnesses, cancer, and even death. Some toxic substances, such as RADON gas, occur naturally, but most are released into the environment because of human activities.

A major group of toxic substances includes *sulphur oxides, nitrogen oxides,* and *carbon monoxide,* airborne chemicals created by the burning of FOSSIL FUELS such as coal, oil, and natural gas. These chemicals are the main contributors to AIR POLLUTION. Sulphur and nitrogen oxides are two components of urban SMOG. Excessive levels of these chemicals can irritate tissues and cause or aggravate respiratory illnesses. Carbon monoxide, released mainly from automobile exhausts, interferes with the blood's ability to carry oxygen. In large concentrations, it can cause death. (See also CARBON MONOXIDE POISONING.)

Another group of toxic substances includes the metals mercury and lead, which are poisonous when eaten or inhaled. Mercury or lead in the food supply can build up in body tissues and cause severe problems. One source of *mercury* poisoning is contaminated fish. In some parts of the world, industrial wastes containing high levels of mercury have been dumped into the oceans. The metal makes its way through the food chain to fish and shellfish, in which it may become highly concentrated. When eaten, the mercury-contaminated fish can cause blindness, paralysis, and even death. Until recently, LEAD was an ingredient in both paint and gasoline. Lead poisoning can cause mental retardation in children.

Mercury in the Environment. *Some experts suggest that people moderate their intake of certain kinds of fish in order to lessen the chance of ingesting mercury, a dangerous toxic substance.*

Other environmental toxins include PCBs, dioxin, and DDT. PCBs (polychlorinated biphenyls) are hydrocarbons used in the manufacture of electrical equipment. They have caused liver and kidney damage, skin lesions, and tumors in laboratory animals. The pesticide DDT (dichlorodiphenyltrichloroethane) was banned in the United States in 1972 because it threatened to destroy wildlife and is harmful to humans. *Dioxin,* a chemical found in some herbicides, is believed to be highly toxic even in very small amounts. Because of the danger of these substances, the United States and other countries continue to struggle over how to reduce their concentration in the air, water, and food chain. (See also ACID RAIN; AGRICULTURAL POLLUTION; HAZARDOUS WASTE; OZONE; PARTICULATES; WATER POLLUTION.)

▶ VIOLENCE

Violence is any act that intentionally causes physical harm to another person. It is a leading cause of INJURY and death in the United States. According to the FBI, more than 23,000 people were murdered, more than 102,000 were raped, and more than 1.6 million were robbed or assaulted in 1990. However, crime experts believe that large numbers of nonfatal rapes and assaults are never reported to law-enforcement agencies, so the actual numbers are probably much higher.

Kinds of Violence Many acts of violence take place within the home. Victims of *domestic violence* are usually women, children, and elderly parents, although men may also be victims. It is estimated that as many as 3 million women and 250,000 men are victims of SPOUSE ABUSE each year and that thousands of husbands and wives are murdered by their spouses annually. CHILD ABUSE is also a major social problem in the United States. More than 2 million cases of child abuse and neglect are reported each year, and as many as 5,000 children die from abuse annually.

Street violence, including HOMICIDE, rape, robbery, and assault, is common in some parts of America. Most such crimes are committed by males younger than the age of 25. Victims of their violence are most likely to be poor and members of minority groups. In fact, for young black males between the ages of 14 and 44, homicide is now the leading cause of death. And young black women are the most common victims of rape.

RISK FACTORS
▶ ▶ ▶ ▶ ▶ ▶

Causes of Violence Poverty, unemployment, divorce, stress, mental illness, and a family history of domestic violence all seem to contribute to violent behavior within the home. People who were abused as children or who grew up in a home where spouse abuse was the norm are more like to become abusers themselves. Abuse is also more common in people who are isolated from their families or from other social support networks.

RISK FACTORS
▶ ▶ ▶ ▶ ▶ ▶

Alcoholism and drug abuse are factors in a large number of violent crimes. Many people are more likely to act violently when under the influence of alcohol. In addition, the buying, selling, and using of illegal drugs has led to an epidemic of violence in America's inner cities. A number of murder victims have been involved in drug dealing; others have been the innocent victims of drug-related *gang violence.*

Some researchers point to depictions of violence in the media as a major contributor to violence. These experts argue that children who see thousands of acts of violence on television or in films each year tend to become used to violence and see it as an acceptable way to solve problems. These children are therefore more likely to become violent themselves. Other experts disagree, noting that the majority of people who are exposed to violence in the media never become violent themselves.

The presence of firearms in many homes may make it easier for people to commit violent acts. Of the more than 23,000 murders that occurred in 1990, almost 13,000 were committed with firearms.

HEALTHY CHOICES

Preventing Violence There are a number of ways that individuals can help protect themselves and their families against violence from strangers. For example, you can protect yourself against assault by keeping your house and car doors locked. Never let a stranger into the house, and never pick up a stranger in your car or accept a ride from a stranger. Avoid walking outside alone at night. Stay clear of alleys, dark doorways, and shrubbery in which an attacker could hide. Park in well-lighted areas, and use main roads as much as possible.

Be aware, though, that many assaults are committed by people with whom the victim is acquainted—not just by strangers. People should avoid being alone with anyone who they think might become violent.

Victims of domestic violence can get help from hot lines and social service agencies. Many communities have shelters and may provide some legal aid for domestic abuse victims. Victims of domestic abuse, rape, and sexual assault can get counseling at community health agencies and volunteer organizations, like Women Against Rape (WAR).

Many people believe that GUN CONTROL and stricter criminal laws could help curb violence in the United States. Others stress the importance of controlling illegal drugs or strengthening social service networks. Recent changes by law-enforcement agencies have made the police more willing to treat spouse abuse as a serious crime and to arrest and prosecute abusers. (See also AGGRESSIVENESS, 5; RAPE, 6; SEXUAL ABUSE, 6.)

▶ **WASTE MANAGEMENT** Waste management refers to coordination of the various methods for dealing with the unwanted by-products of industrial and human activities, such as HAZARDOUS WASTE, SEWAGE, and SOLID WASTE. During the twentieth century, the quantity of waste materials has increased dramatically as a result of industrialization and POPULATION GROWTH. In addition, many waste materials today are more toxic than those of the past. As a result, nearly all nations of the world now face an urgent dilemma of how to dispose of waste materials without endangering human health or the environment. Doing so is the major goal of comprehensive waste management.

Common methods of waste disposal include landfills, incineration (controlled burning at high temperatures), and chemical treatment. Hazardous wastes, which include harmful chemicals and radioactive wastes, present special problems because of their toxicity. In recent years, governments and individuals have sought to manage waste through more

A Throwaway Society. *Americans create vast amounts of waste every day, and finding ways to dispose of it safely is a growing concern for governments and individuals.*

efficient production processes that produce fewer unwanted by-products. RECYCLING, or processing waste material for reuse, is another promising method of waste management. (See also AIR POLLUTION; SANITATION; TOXIC SUBSTANCES; WATER POLLUTION.)

> ## WATER CONSERVATION
Water conservation is any action that a government or an individual takes to avoid wasting water or to prevent it from becoming contaminated. All humans, animals, and plants need water to survive. Humans need clean, fresh water for domestic, agricultural, and industrial uses. They use water for drinking, cooking, and bathing; to irrigate crops; and to operate factories.

Fresh water is an abundant natural resource, but it is not distributed evenly. In some places, rainfall and water supplies are scarce; others have more than they need to support the population. Parts of the United States face serious water shortages. To add to this problem, more and more water sources are becoming polluted.

Public Water Conservation Methods   Water can be conserved in many ways. Many municipalities maintain reservoirs for their water supply. *Reservoirs* may be natural lakes or artificial bodies of water created by building dams on rivers or streams. Some communities obtain their water supplies from *groundwater,* the natural supply of water underground. Some groundwater is found in *aquifers,* which are large, natural underground reservoirs.

In arid regions, *aqueducts* may be used to transport water to communities from distant lakes or rivers. Snow runoff and rainwater may also be captured to replenish water supplies. *Watersheds* are planned areas of vegetation that trap rainwater so that it can soak into the ground, renewing groundwater supplies. Watersheds can also help to control flooding and erosion. (See also WEATHER-RELATED EMERGENCIES.)

Preventing WATER POLLUTION is another aspect of water conservation. Certain chemicals used in fertilizers and pesticides can contaminate water runoff, eventually fouling lakes and rivers. Lakes and oceans may also be polluted with untreated or inadequately treated sewage or with industrial

Preventing Waste. *Taking shorter showers is an easy way for people to save many gallons of water.*

wastes. Polluted water can cause a variety of health problems, from minor intestinal disorders to a greater risk of contracting certain kinds of cancer. (See also AGRICULTURAL POLLUTION; THERMAL POLLUTION; WATER PURITY.)

Individual Water Conservation Methods   Individuals can save thousands of gallons of water in their own homes each year by using water conservation methods. Gallons of household water are wasted every day when people leave water running as they wash dishes, shave, or brush their teeth. Installing water-saving showerheads and toilets and promptly repairing leaky pipes and faucets will also conserve water. Using appliances like dishwashers and washing machines only when they are full also saves water. In addition, proper disposal of oil and other dangerous chemicals helps prevent pollution of water supplies. By supporting water conservation methods, individuals can help ensure that there will be a safe and abundant water supply available for everyone in the future.

► WATER POLLUTION

Water pollution can be defined as any physical or chemical change in water that upsets the natural balance of aquatic life. Common pollutants include untreated human and animal wastes, industrial chemicals, pesticides, and petroleum products.

In addition to reducing the amount of water available for household, agricultural, and manufacturing needs, water pollution is associated with a variety of human health problems. People who drink water contaminated with SEWAGE may develop diseases like cholera and dysentery. When released into oceans, lakes, streams, and sources of groundwater, TOXIC SUBSTANCES may enter the food chain. Depending on the amounts ingested, these chemicals may cause reproductive-system disorders, cancer, and even death.

Types of Water Pollution   Certain kinds of water pollution occur naturally. The natural decay of plants and animals along with leaching of minerals from soil, for example, pollutes water. Human and animal waste products are also a source of pollution.

Many pollutants, however, are a result of modern technology. These include toxic substances that leach from landfills or that are released as a result of industrial or agricultural processes. Such substances include metals such as mercury and LEAD; fertilizer and pesticide residues; PCBs (polychlorinated biphenyls); and oil (see chart: Common Water Pollutants and Their Sources). Waterways may also be harmed by power plants that use water for cooling. Dumping heated water into a waterway is known as THERMAL POLLUTION. Another type of water pollution is ACID RAIN, formed when substances released from the burning of FOSSIL FUELS combine with moisture in the air and return to bodies of water as rain or runoff.

Effects of Water Pollution   Drinking water that has been contaminated by human and animal wastes can lead to diseases like cholera and typhoid fever. Modern sewage treatment facilities, designed to remove most disease-causing microorganisms from the water supply, have greatly reduced the incidence of these diseases in industrialized countries. In

COMMON WATER POLLUTANTS AND THEIR SOURCES		
Type	**Pollutant**	**Sources**
Biological	Bacteria, viruses, protozoa	Human and animal wastes
	Nitrates and phosphates	Fertilizer runoff from agriculture
		Animal wastes
		Inadequate sewage treatment
		Some detergents
Metals	Arsenic	Insecticides
	Lead	Lead-based paint
		Lead pipes
		Leaded gasoline
	Cadmium	Industrial wastes
		Old galvanized pipes
		Insecticides
	Mercury	Industrial wastes
		Agricultural wastes
Others	Asbestos	Asbestos/cement water pipes
	Chlorinated hydrocarbons (DDT, chlordane, Kepone)	Pesticides
	Acid rain	Combustion of fossil fuels
	Oil	Tanker spills
		Seepage from underground tanks and deposits
	PCBs (polychlorinated biphenyls)	Manufacture of transformers and other electrical equipment

many parts of the world, however, water polluted with human and animal wastes is still common.

In the United States, pollution from agricultural and industrial chemicals is a bigger problem. For example, nitrates and phosphates from fertilizers may get into a body of water. There they cause aquatic plants to grow very quickly, then die and decay. The decaying process uses up much of the oxygen in the water, causing fish and other animals to suffocate. This depletion of oxygen, called *eutrophication*, can also occur because of thermal pollution.

Toxic chemicals are especially dangerous because of their ability to enter the food chain. Many of these chemicals become more and more concentrated as they move higher up the food chain. When people consume fish that have been contaminated with mercury, mercury poisoning may result. Mercury poisoning can cause serious nervous system damage as well as mental retardation and physical deformities in children. Chlorinated hydrocarbons are chemicals found in runoff from pesticides such as chlordane, Kepone, and DDT (now banned in the United States). Ingestion of these substances has been linked to cancer, birth defects, and reproductive-system disorders. PCB-contaminated drinking water has been associated with kidney and liver damage.

Certain types of water pollution are especially harmful to wildlife. Oil spills can kill marine mammals, fish, sea birds, and aquatic plants and make beaches unfit for recreational use. Acid rain can kill plant and animal life, and the substances that create it may also contribute to human respiratory problems.

Reducing Water Pollution Within the past several decades, the United States government has taken a number of important steps to clean up the nation's waterways. Some programs allow officials to monitor the release of substances and trace certain contaminants to their sources. Legislation has been introduced to help protect aquifers (natural collection areas for groundwater) from chemicals and other pollutants. Runoff from farms, roadways, and households is much more difficult to control. In addition, *ocean dumping* of sewage sludge continues in some areas, posing serious risks to both swimmers and wildlife. (See also AGRICULTURAL POLLUTION; OIL SPILLS; SANITATION; WATER PURITY.)

▶ **WATER PURITY** Water purity, or the cleanliness and safety of drinking water, is an important public health concern. A variety of methods are used to remove disease-causing bacteria from the water supply. In recent years, however, concern has grown about certain contaminants, such as agricultural chemicals, that are not filtered out by traditional water purification methods.

Testing for Bacteria Public health officials check the purity of drinking water by monitoring the number of *coliform bacteria* present in it. Coliform bacteria are present in fecal matter. They are not necessarily dangerous in themselves, but when they are found in the water supply, it is an indication that other, more dangerous, bacteria are also likely to be present. National standards require that in any one month, the average number of coliform bacteria per test be less than 1 bacterium per 100 mL of water. Water may also be tested for the presence of other pollutants.

Water Treatment Water is usually collected in a reservoir or pumped from an underground source. It is then purified by a number of processes, including forcing it through special equipment to remove unwanted gases. The process of *sedimentation* allows solid material to sink to the bottom and be removed. A final filtering through a substance such as gravel or charcoal removes further impurities along with tastes and odors. Finally, water usually goes through *chlorination*, in which the chemical chlorine is added to the water to kill remaining bacteria.

Principal Stages in Water Purification.

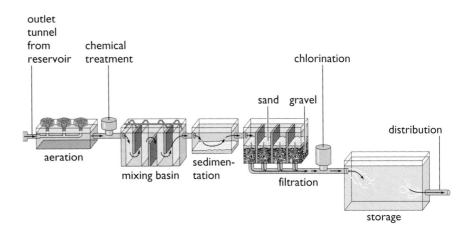

outlet tunnel from reservoir / chemical treatment / chlorination / sand / gravel / distribution / aeration / mixing basin / sedimentation / filtration / storage

> Concerns about the purity of tap water have prompted some people to switch to bottled water. Some bottled products, however, contain the same pollutants that tap water does.

Concerns About the Water Supply Although traditional water treatment processes remove many dangerous pathogens, increased quantities of chemical pollutants in the public water supply have caused widespread concern. The intensive use of fertilizers and other agricultural chemicals, for example, has resulted in nitrate contamination of some underground aquifers, and these contaminants are difficult to remove. (See also AGRICULTURAL POLLUTION.)

In many areas, concerns about the purity of tap water have prompted people to switch to *bottled water.* (This term can refer to distilled water, mineral water, seltzer, sparkling water, club soda, and spring water.) Some bottled products, however, contain the same pollutants that tap water does. Others are high in sodium and inorganic chemicals. Bottled waters do not necessarily, therefore, offer any real health benefits except in areas where the local tap water is seriously polluted. (See also SEWAGE; WATER CONSERVATION; WATER POLLUTION.)

▶ WATER SAFETY

Every year, thousands of Americans drown and many more are injured in swimming, boating, and diving accidents. In fact, DROWNING is the third most common cause of accidental death after motor vehicle accidents and falls. Practicing a few safety rules when swimming, boating, and diving can help avoid many injuries and deaths in the water.

The most important rule for enjoying water sports safely is to learn to swim before engaging in any water sport. Nearly everyone can learn how to swim, even people with physical disabilities. Virtually every community has supervised facilities, such as YMCA/YWCA, the Red Cross, and community centers, where people can learn to swim.

HEALTHY CHOICES

A second important rule is to avoid drinking alcohol while engaging in water sports. Alcohol affects judgment, slows reflexes, and dulls the senses. Just as with automobile accidents, many boating accidents involve boat operators—as well as passengers—who have been drinking. Swimmers who have been drinking are likely to take dangerous chances, and they are also at increased risk of HYPOTHERMIA.

Swimming Safety It is best to swim in areas protected by lifeguards. If a lifeguard is not in the area, swim with a companion and keep an eye on one another. Swimmers should also know their own limits. Even the most experienced swimmers can be overpowered by strong *undertows* or *currents*, and strong swimmers can be incapacitated by muscle *cramping*.

Swimmers should never dive into water without first checking its depth and making sure that there are no rocks or other underwater obstacles. A good rule to remember is "if you can stand in it, don't dive in it."

If a swimmer is drowning or in trouble, it is recommended that only a trained lifeguard or person who has taken an approved *lifesaving course* swim out to perform a rescue. Others should throw something that floats, extend a rope or pole, or row a boat out to the swimmer. In some cases, CPR (cardiopulmonary resuscitation) may be needed to revive rescued swimmers.

People with backyard swimming pools should encourage *pool safety* by following basic safety rules. One of the most important rules is never

Life Jackets. *Boaters should make a point of always wearing life jackets as a safety precaution.*

leave a child alone in or near a pool even for a moment. Most communities require that private pools be fenced in behind a locked gate.

Boating Safety   Before going out in any boat, the operator must become completely familiar with how to operate it as well as with the boating regulations in the area. Yachting clubs and the U.S. Coast Guard offer courses in boat safety and handling for beginners.

Every person on board a boat should wear a *life jacket* at all times. Every boat should carry flares and a fire extinguisher and be equipped with navigation lights. Larger boats are required to carry a horn or whistle. Boats that travel out of sight of the shoreline should also have an emergency signaling device, which indicates the boat's location, a flashlight that floats, emergency fuel, and an automatic bailing pump and bailing buckets.

If a boat capsizes, passengers should not attempt to swim to shore. It is easier to spot an overturned boat in the water than a lone swimmer. The boat also provides something to hang on to or sit on until help comes. If the boat sinks, debris such as seat cushions and ice chests can be used to hold onto until help comes.

Water skiers should check all equipment carefully before going out and always wear life jackets. They should never ski in shallow water and must watch the water for unexpected obstacles. Water skiers should never wrap the rope or handle around a hand or foot. Ski boat operators are important also. The driver of the boat must maneuver the boat smoothly while avoiding swimmers, rocks, buoys, and other boats, and a passenger in the boat must interpret the skier's hand signals for the driver.

Underwater Diving Safety   Underwater divers must take lessons from a qualified instructor before they are allowed to purchase diving equipment and dive. Divers should always check the equipment carefully before descending to make sure it is in good working order. A timer and depth gauge are two essential pieces of equipment. Divers should be in good health. They should not dive if their eustachian tubes are blocked from colds or flu; these tubes must be able to open as the diver descends to prevent rupturing the eardrums.

Divers should always dive with a companion so they can help each other in case of trouble. They must surface slowly from great depths to avoid the BENDS, or decompression sickness, an accumulation of nitrogen in the bloodstream that can cause convulsions and death. (See also ACCIDENTS.)

▶ **WEATHER-RELATED EMERGENCIES**   Weather-related emergencies include health hazards caused by heat and drought, thunderstorms, tornadoes, hurricanes, floods, and cold and blizzards. Health risks and safety precautions for weather conditions depend on the specific type of emergency.

Heat and Drought   During very hot weather, HEATSTROKE is a health risk, especially for older people and those who exercise vigorously. Heatstroke, a failure of the body's temperature regulation system, is an acute emergency that requires immediate medical treatment.

CONSULT A
PHYSICIAN

A number of additional health problems can occur during hot, dry weather. High concentrations of OZONE and other forms of AIR POLLUTION can cause respiratory problems, especially among young children, older people, and those with respiratory disease. Forest fires, more prevalent in drought conditions, can damage property and cause injury and death. Dry conditions can also lead to reduced or contaminated drinking-water supplies.

Thunderstorms   During a thunderstorm, lightning can cause fatalities or severe BURNS. Lightning rods can protect a house from lightning. If a house has no lightning rod, occupants should stay away from metal objects, the telephone, plumbing, the fireplace, and open doors and windows during a storm. Individuals who are caught outside during a storm should avoid anything in the landscape that could act as a lightning rod, such as a lone tree, a wire fence, or an open boat. They should seek shelter in a low-lying spot. If someone is struck by lightning, breathing and heartbeat should be checked immediately, and CPR (cardiopulmonary resuscitation) should be provided if needed.

Tornadoes   Tornadoes, also called twisters or cyclones, are powerful, twisting storms with winds as high as 300 miles (483 km) per hour. About 750 tornadoes occur in the United States each year, killing and injuring hundreds of people. The months of April through June are the peak periods for tornadoes, which often strike with little or no warning. When weather conditions indicate the possibility of severe storms, stay tuned to the radio or television for advisory bulletins. Keep a battery-powered radio and flashlights on hand in case of power loss.

The main risk in a tornado is being picked up by the wind or struck with flying debris. In the event of a tornado, a person should take shelter in a basement or cellar and stay away from the windows. In a building without a basement, the best place to go is to an interior room on the lowest level of the building. Anyone who is caught outside should go to the interior of the nearest building. Never stay in a car or truck. If no shelter is available, lie flat in a ditch or ravine.

Tornadoes.   *When the funnel-shaped cloud of a tornado touches down, its powerful winds destroy everything in its path.*

Hurricanes   These powerful, swirling rainstorms often measure hundreds of miles in diameter and carry winds that blow between 74 and 150 miles (119 and 240 km) per hour. Severe hurricanes cause millions of dollars in property damage as well as injury and death. The National Weather Service tracks developing storms to determine which ones may develop into hurricanes. Its data help predict where a hurricane will hit and how strong it will be. Adequate warning is usually given so that residents can vacate areas in the path of a hurricane. Leaving for an inland area is the most prudent course when a hurricane is approaching.

Floods   Hurricanes, storms, tidal waves, and heavy rainfall can result in flooding that destroys homes and buildings, disrupts utility and phone services, and causes injury and death. When weather conditions indicate possible flooding, it is advisable to stay tuned to the radio or television for warnings and instructions. If warnings do occur, turn off electrical and other services and head for higher ground. After the waters recede, buildings that were flooded need to be decontaminated before they can be used again. Water supplies are often contaminated as well.

Cold and Blizzards   FROSTBITE, especially of fingers, toes, face, and ears, is a common injury in cold weather because the body sends less blood to the hands and feet in order to conserve heat for its vital internal organs. Warm clothing, especially on the head, face, hands, and feet, is the best protection against frostbite during cold-weather activities. It is also wise to be aware of the wind-chill factor and take regular breaks to go indoors to warm up.

HEALTHY CHOICES

Blizzards are snowstorms with very cold winds of 35 miles (56 km) per hour or more and limited visibility. The safest place to be during a blizzard is indoors. Anyone who must be outside is advised to wear protective clothing, including thermal undergarments; wind- and moisture-repellent outer garments; head, face, and ear coverings; extra socks; warm boots; and lined mittens. Because it is easy to get lost in a blizzard, follow a road or a fence to the closest safe place. (See also EARTHQUAKES; HYPOTHERMIA.)

HEALTHY CHOICES

WOUNDS

Wounds include any damage to the skin or tissues under the skin. In open wounds, the skin or mucous membrane is broken; in closed wounds, the skin or mucous membrane remains intact. Wounds can be caused by ACCIDENTS, surgery, or a violent act.

Types of Wounds   A *contusion,* or bruise, is a closed wound in which underlying tissue is damaged but the skin is not broken. An *abrasion* involves damage to the outer layer of skin, with little or no bleeding. An *incision* is an open wound made by a knife or other sharp object. It may cause heavy bleeding and damage to muscle and nerve tissues. A *laceration* is a jagged, irregular tear in the skin. It too may cause heavy bleeding, and it carries a high risk of infection and underlying tissue damage. A *puncture wound* may occur when a nail, splinter, bullet, or other object pierces the skin. Although there may be little external bleeding, a puncture wound can cause internal bleeding and organ damage and carries a high risk of infection. An *avulsion* is a wound that causes tissue to be separated from the body. Animal bites and automobile accidents may result in avulsions.

Wound First Aid   The main objectives of FIRST AID for wounds are to stop BLEEDING and prevent infection. Minor wounds can be treated by washing thoroughly with soap and water to remove any dirt. Scrapes and scratches can be left exposed to the air; larger wounds should be covered with a sterile dressing. (Anyone providing first aid to a person who is bleeding should wash his or her hands before and after giving aid and wear rubber gloves whenever possible to prevent the spread of infection.) Any wound that is large or deep, continues to bleed, or shows signs of infection requires medical attention. Treatment may include suturing (stitching), specialized surgical techniques, and administration of antibiotics to fight infection. (See also BITES AND STINGS; INJURIES; TETANUS, **2.**)

CONSULT A
PHYSICIAN

SUPPLEMENTARY SOURCES

American Medical Association. 1990. *Handbook of first aid and emergency care.* New York: Random House.

American Red Cross. 1992. *First aid and safety handbook.* Boston: Little, Brown.

American Red Cross. 1991. *First aid responding to emergencies.* St. Louis: Mosby Year Book.

Anders, Madelyn K. 1987. *Environmental diseases.* New York: Franklin Watts.

Anderson, Bruce N. 1991. *Ecologue: The environmental catalogue and consumer's guide for a safe earth.* New York: Prentice-Hall Press.

Auerbach, Paul S. 1986. *Medicine for the outdoors: A guide to emergency medical procedures and first aid.* Boston: Little, Brown.

Baldwin, J. 1990. *Whole earth ecolog: The best of environmental tools and ideas.* New York: Crown.

Bowman, Warren D. 1988. *Outdoor emergency care.* Denver: National Ski Patrol.

Brown, Lester R. 1992. *State of the world: 1992. Worldwatch Institute report on progress toward a sustainable society.* Updated annually. New York: Norton.

Carson, Rachel. 1962. *Silent spring.* Burlington, Mass.: Houghton Mifflin.

Commoner, Barry. 1990. *Making peace with the planet.* New York: Pantheon.

Dodd, Debra Lynn. 1986. *The nontoxic house: Protecting yourself and your family from everyday toxics and health hazards.* Los Angeles: J. P. Tarcher.

Ehrlich, Paul. 1970. *The population bomb.* New York: Ballantine Books.

Fisher, David E. 1990. *Fire and ice: The greenhouse effect, ozone depletion, and nuclear winter.* New York: Harper & Row.

Gabler, Raymond, and the editors of Consumer Reports. 1988. *Is your water safe to drink?* Mt. Vernon, N.Y.: Consumers Union.

Kittredge, Mary. 1991. *Emergency medicine.* New York: Chelsea House.

Lentz, Martha J., Steven C. Macdonald, and Jan D. Carline. 1985. *Mountaineering first aid: A guide to accident response and first aid care.* 3d ed. Seattle: The Mountaineers.

Levine, Michael. 1991. *The environmental address book: How to reach the environment's greatest champions and worst offenders.* New York: Perigree Books.

National Safety Council. 1992. *Accident facts.* Updated annually. Chicago: National Safety Council.

Schneider, Stephen H. 1989. *Global warming: Are we entering the greenhouse century?* San Francisco: Sierra Club Books.

Seredich, John, ed. 1991. *Your resource guide to environmental organizations.* Irvine, Calif.: Smiling Dolphins Press.

Szczawinski, Adam, and Nancy J. Turner. 1991. *Common poisonous plants and mushrooms of North America.* Portland, Ore.: Timber Press.

University of California, Berkeley. 1991. *The wellness encyclopedia.* Boston: Houghton Mifflin.

ORGANIZATIONS

AAA Foundation for Traffic Safety
1730 M Street, NW
Washington, DC 20036
(202) 775-1456

American Heart Association
7320 Greenville Avenue
Dallas, TX 75231
(214) 373-6300

American Medical Association
515 North State Street
Chicago, IL 60610
(312) 464-5000

American Red Cross
National Headquarters
Seventeenth and D Streets, NW
Washington, DC 20006
(202) 737-8300

American Public Health Association
1015 Fifteenth Street, NW
Washington, DC 20005
(202) 789-5600

Center for Population Options
1025 Vermont Avenue, NW
Suite 210
Washington, DC 20005
(202) 347-5700

Clearinghouse on Child Abuse and Neglect Information
P.O. Box 1182
Washington, DC 20013
(703) 385-7565

Consumer Product Safety Commission
National Injury Information Clearinghouse
Washington, DC 20207
(301) 504-0580

Environmental Protection Agency
Public Information Center
401 M Street, SW
Washington, DC 20460
(202) 260-2090

Friends of the Earth
218 D Street, SE
Washington, DC 20003
(202) 544-2600

Greenpeace, U.S.A.
1436 U Street, NW
Washington, DC 20009
(202) 462-1177

Medic Alert Foundation International
2323 Colorado Avenue
Turlock, CA 95380
(209) 668-3333

National Audubon Society
950 Third Avenue
New York, NY 10022
(212) 832-3200

National Committee for the Prevention of Child Abuse
332 South Michigan Avenue
Chicago, IL 60604
(312) 663-3520

National Emergency Medicine Association
306 West Joppa Road
Towson, MD 21204
(301) 494-0300

National Highway Traffic Safety Administration
Department of Transportation
400 Seventh Avenue, SW
Washington, DC 20590
Auto Safety Hot Line
(202) 366-0123

National Institute of Environmental
Health Sciences
P.O. Box 12233
Research Triangle Park, NC 27709
(919) 541-3345

National Institute for Occupational
Safety and Health
Centers for Disease Control
1600 Clifton Road, NE
Atlanta, GA 30333
(404) 639-3061

National Safety Council
1121 Spring Lake Drive
Itasca, IL 60143
(708) 285-1121

National Ski Patrol System
133 South Van Gordon Street
Lakewood, CO 80228
(303) 988-1111

National Wildlife Federation
1400 Sixteenth Street, NW
Washington, DC 20036
(202) 797-6800

Occupational Safety and Health
Administration (OSHA)
U.S. Department of Labor
200 Constitution Avenue, NW
Washington, DC 20210
(202) 219-8148

Sierra Club
730 Polk Street
San Francisco, CA 94109
(415) 776-2211

Worldwatch Institute
1776 Massachusetts Avenue, NW
Washington, DC 20036
(202) 452-1999

INDEX

Italicized page numbers refer to illustrations or charts.